waste not

waste not

recipes and tips for full-use
cooking from america's best chefs
james beard foundation
photography by keirnan monaghan
and theo vamvounakis

RIZZOLI NEW YORK

New York · Paris · London · Milan

When I was growing up, cooking in our house in Elizabeth, New Jersey, was a family affair. My brothers and I ate food prepared by parents, grandparents, aunts and uncles, all of whom were children of the Great Depression or immigrants, or both— people who had personally known hard times, even hunger. Thrift was a virtue little discussed and much practiced: Heels of stale bread became bread crumbs. Leftover veggies were tossed into a frittata (we called it an omelet). Last night's meatloaf was the next day's sandwich.

In restaurant parlance, thrift is called good management; bones are harvested for flavor, carrot tops go into stock. Profit margins are slender in our industry even in the best of times, so almost nothing of value gets thrown out. Shrewd husbandry and imaginative use of the "imperfect extra" can be the difference between keeping the lights on or not.

But for those of us who don't work in restaurants or have a direct connection to a leaner past, the idea of this kind of careful waste management feels quaint at best, and onerous at worst, given the demands of our frenetic family and work lives. *Who's got time to make stock? I recycle, now I'm supposed to compost, too?* We've come of age in an era of low-cost fast food and convenience meals, with many layers of processing and packaging between us and the human beings that cultivated the ingredients in them. It's that distance, real and metaphorical, that makes waste possible: throwing away half of a dollar meal is easier than tossing half the ragu your grandmother made from scratch, or half of a crop your family labored to grow.

Today, most of us see the role we play, as individuals, in safeguarding the environment. We recycle, and we make consumer decisions based on energy efficiency and carbon footprint, because we understand the collective impact of those choices on our swiftly warming planet.

But we do that while letting our leftovers grow fur in the fridge before tossing them. While crumpling the last two fingers of sandwich in our lunch bag and flipping vegetable scraps into a garbage pile destined for a landfill, without connecting the dots: if food waste were its own country, it would be the world's third-largest producer of greenhouse gases. Twenty-five percent of all the fresh water in the U.S. is used to produce food that is wasted. The hidden costs of food waste jack up food costs across the board, which hits low-income families the hardest. Forty percent of all the food produced in the U.S. gets thrown away in a nation where one in six people go hungry. In that light, those small moments of mindless waste have staggering consequences.

The good news is that each of us can help fix this. Scraps can be frozen until a later date and then tossed into a pot for stock. Bits and ends of lunch can be collected for compost. Just a fifteen percent reduction in food waste could save enough food to feed twenty-five million Americans annually. It's heartening, too, to think of the generational impact on our children of learning thrift-by-choice. Kids who grow up scraping their plates into a compost bin will do so in their own households one day; for their kids, throwing away food scraps will feel the way that tossing a tin can into anything but the recycling bin feels to ours: an act from the dark ages, like smoking on airplanes, or hurling your picnic trash out a car window. These behaviors were normal when I was a kid. But norms change when we decide to live our lives with intent, and help others to do the same.

This book is for the eater with intent. It's for the home cook who hopes to lean into this issue but needs ideas for how to pull it off, how to manage or transform that bit of "imperfect extra" that is the by-product of daily life. Change can be delicious, it can be fun, and it can become habit. And small habits, adopted by many, can tip a culture from indifference and neglect toward a saner, more just future in which we all can share. Thanks for being part of getting us there.

TOM COLICCHIO
NEW YORK CITY, 2018

Decades ago, long before the farm-to-table movement, cookbook author and culinary educator James Beard wrote, "It is true thrift to use the best ingredients available and to waste nothing."

**A NOTE FROM THE
JAMES BEARD FOUNDATION**

Beard, the inspiration behind the James Beard Foundation and the James Beard Awards, was nurtured and nourished by his mother, Elizabeth Beard, who was an excellent cook herself, in Portland, Oregon, during the early 1900s. Amid the Pacific Northwest's seasonal abundance, Beard learned that to waste food was to waste culinary potential—indeed, to waste flavor.

A century has passed since James Beard's childhood, and with all that we have learned about food and cooking from our favorite chefs and from Beard's many cookbooks, there is one maxim that we could adhere to better in our home kitchens: waste not.

In restaurant kitchens around the country, chefs use ingredients that home cooks often discard—from onion scraps to carrot tops, from fish bones to chicken fat—to build layers of flavor and keep purchased products from being wasted. The result? Two outcomes that are pretty irresistible to chefs: lower food costs and more flavorful dishes.

In our own homes, the numbers tell a different story. According to the Natural Resources Defense Council, a quarter of the food we purchase ends up in the garbage, which means that the average American household is throwing away more than $1,500 worth of food each year. And the problem has gotten worse: in the early twenty-first century, we waste three times as much food as we did in 1950, when Beard was in his prime.

Unlike the centuries-old culinary traditions of France, Italy, Japan, or any ancient food system, for that matter, cooks in the United States haven't developed the deep repertoire of dishes that use up agricultural and culinary by-products to full gastronomic effect. The *fromage de tête* and *pied de porc* of France, the minestrone and *pappa al pomodoro* of Italy, the kimchi and *doenjang* of Korea, and other dishes the world over that form the gastronomic heart of these rich culinary identities are often repositories for ingredients and scraps that would otherwise be wasted.

Celebrated chef and ecological cooking advocate Dan Barber repeatedly reminds us of the systems that purposely use the by-product of one thing to support the production of another: pigs that make the famous hams of Italy's Parma region are fed the whey leftover from the production of the region's other great offering, Parmigiano-Reggiano. This is not coincidence; it is synergy.

At the James Beard Foundation, we believe that one of the most important things we can do to stem the flow of wasted food is make flavor the solution. To generate more interest in ingredients that aren't traditionally given starring roles, we turned to our most trusted resources: chefs.

Nobody knows more about how to fully utilize every last leaf, root, bone, stem, and rind than chefs—both out of respect for the ingredients themselves and to meet their bottom lines. Nobody has more recipes and tips for home cooks about how to make their food dollars go further and their dishes more flavorful. And nobody has more influence in the way that America cooks than the chefs who have become trendsetters and tastemakers alike.

Since 2012, more than 200 chefs from around the country have participated in the James Beard Foundation's Chefs Boot Camp for Policy and Change, participating in food-system advocacy training focused on a number of topics, including how they can help reduce food waste in America. The ideas, recipes, and cooking philosophies in this book come from this passionate group of chef advocates.

To these chefs, waste is a matter of perspective. They don't see root tops, bones, scraps, and seeds as garbage, necessarily—they see them as ingredients, building blocks of cuisine, many of them part of long-standing cultural traditions, and all of them an opportunity to create new dishes and build layers of flavor. So we started to wonder: What if we all changed our perspective in this way? How much food could be diverted from landfills? How much further could our groceries go? How much money could we save? And how much more delicious could our food be?

We hope that the creative and instructional recipes and tips that these chefs have shared in *Waste Not* will inspire you to see the beauty, utility, and possibilities in all and every part of our food.

Cooking

from this book

This book is divided into five sections, each featuring different kinds of recipes that reduce food waste. The first chapter, "From Stem to Stem," features recipes that use all of the parts of fruits and vegetables—for example, beet burgers that use the roasted beets, beet greens, and pickled stems, and an orange cake that utilizes the whole orange, pith and all. The second chapter, "Meat, Bones, Skin & Scales," features nose-to-tail recipes for chicken, fish, and other animals, but also recipes that highlight the unique potential of by-products of proteins, like whey-cooked grains that showcase the unique flavor of the often-discarded acidic liquid left after the production of cheese and Greek yogurt. In "Tops & Bottoms, Pits & Peels," you'll find recipes and ideas for the tops, bottoms, peels, and other pieces of ingredients you're often left with after you make something else, from radish and carrot tops to grapefruit peels and pineapple skins. "Second-Day Solutions" is filled with ideas for new dishes to create from your leftovers: takeout rice, last night's brisket and mashed potatoes, and even day-old doughnuts. The last chapter, "Prolonged & Preserved," is all about saving ingredients from the compost bin, from bruised avocados to overripe berries, and also features techniques like fermenting, pickling, and other ways to turbo boost both the flavor and shelf life of your ingredients.

Each chapter begins with tips that the chefs use in their restaurants and their homes to cut down on waste. Ideas range from saving scraps in the freezer until you have enough to make stock, to sautéing wilted salad greens for a quick weeknight side dish—more inspiration to take you beyond the recipes in this book.

1.

From Stem to Stem

Tips

1   There is no need to chop off spring
     onion roots or carrot roots—they can
     be beautiful as an element in the dish
     and remind everyone that vegetables
     come from the earth.

2   The tops of root vegetables such
     as carrots, turnips, and radishes are
     wonderfully bitter and are good
     cooked as a vegetable or in a soup.

3   Roast wilting celery and carrots to
     bring them back to life, and then mix
     in scrambled eggs or top them with
     a fried egg for breakfast.

4   Rather than peeling carrots,
     cucumbers, and other vegetables and
     fruits, leave the peels on and give
     them a good scrub to remove any dirt.

5   If you do decide to peel, save the
     scraps for vegetable stocks or
     fruit jams, like those in the Scraps
     chapter on page 84.

6   Save asparagus bottoms, carrot tops, mushroom stems, and other vegetable parts in freezer bags or containers for use in stocks, soups, and sauces.

7   Before wilting herbs turn black, puree them with a little oil and store in ice cube trays or other containers in the freezer so that in the dead of winter, you can grab some bright greens from your freezer.

8   When salad greens start to wilt, sauté them with some olive oil and garlic for a bright side dish.

9   Sauté root vegetable tops and greens to serve as a side dish.

10   To prolong the life of a bunch of ripe
      bananas for future use, place them on
      a sheet pan (skins intact) and bake in
      the oven for 15 minutes at 350°F until
      the skins are a deep black. Once cool,
      peel the roasted bananas and freeze
      in a ziplock bag. They won't darken
      in the freezer, and they're perfect for
      smoothies and banana bread.

11   If you have just a few berries
      or strawberries you want to salvage
      before they turn, lay them out in
      a single layer on a small sheet pan
      or plate. Freeze uncovered overnight,
      then put them in a resealable
      plastic bag and return to the freezer.
      By freezing them separately, you
      can easily pluck them out just a
      few at a time and put them straight
      in the bottom of your bowl before
      topping with hot oatmeal, or add to
      a smoothie for more texture.

Whole
Carrot–Lentil Salad

This recipe highlights the various flavors and textures the humble carrot has to offer, from crunchy raw rounds, to caramelized roasted pieces, to the plentiful and often discarded herbaceous green tops.

YIELD: 4 SERVINGS

CARROTS AND LENTILS:
1 bunch carrots, tops reserved for pesto
2 tablespoons olive oil, divided
2 teaspoons kosher salt
1 teaspoon Aleppo chile flakes, divided
½ teaspoon cumin seeds
Black pepper to taste
½ red onion, chopped
1 cup black lentils, rinsed
2 cups water
4–5 sprigs cilantro, chopped
4–5 sprigs mint, chopped
4–5 sprigs parsley, chopped

TOASTED SEEDS:
½ cup pumpkin seeds
½ cup sunflower seeds
½ teaspoon olive oil

VINAIGRETTE:
Zest and juice of ½ lemon
Zest and juice of ½ tangerine or orange
¼ cup olive oil or canola oil
1 tablespoon white wine vinegar
1 teaspoon honey
½ teaspoon orange flower water
   (optional)

¼ teaspoon salt
Black pepper to taste

CARROT TOP PESTO:
2 cups carrot top leaves (tops of 1 bunch
   of carrots)
2–4 cloves garlic
½ cup olive oil
½ cup toasted pumpkin and sunflower
   seeds from recipe above
Salt to taste

Prepare the carrots: preheat the oven to 350°F. Slice half the carrots into thin coins and set in cold water. Refrigerate.

Cut the other half of the carrots into ½-inch rounds and place them on a baking sheet. Toss the carrots with 1 tablespoon olive oil, 1 teaspoon kosher salt, ½ teaspoon Aleppo chile, cumin seeds, and a little black pepper. Cover the baking sheet with foil and roast the carrots in the oven for 20 minutes. Remove the foil and, if carrots are not browned, broil for 2 to 3 minutes until caramelized. Remove from oven and set aside.

Prepare the lentils: In a medium saucepot, heat the remaining 1 tablespoon olive oil over medium heat. Add the red onion and cook for about 2 minutes or until translucent. Add the lentils and 2 cups water; lower heat to simmer. Cook for 20 to 30 minutes, or until the lentils are tender, adding more water as necessary. Season with the remaining salt, Aleppo chile, and black pepper, to taste. Set aside.

Prepare the toasted seeds: lower the oven to 325°F. Toss all of the ingredients together on a baking sheet and toast the seeds, stirring them every 5 minutes. Cook until the seeds smell nutty and are golden brown, about 15 minutes total.

Make the vinaigrette: whisk or blend all of the ingredients together. Set aside.

Prepare the pesto: blanch the carrot top leaves and garlic in boiling water for 30 seconds. Drain and rinse under cold water, squeezing out the moisture from the carrot tops. Combine the blanched carrot top leaves and garlic, olive oil, and toasted seeds with a pinch of salt in a blender. Check the seasoning.

To serve, drain the raw carrot coins well and toss in a large bowl with ¼ cup vinaigrette. Add the roasted carrots and toss again. Add the lentils and a bit more of the vinaigrette and gently toss to combine.

Place about ½ cup of pesto on a plate and top with lentils and carrot salad. Sprinkle on the remaining toasted seeds and garnish with the cilantro, mint, and parsley.

Grilled Asparagus

with
Asparagus-Bottom Aïoli

Springtime in restaurants means lots of asparagus on menus, and piles of rubber band–wrapped asparagus bottoms lingering in the kitchen. But by poaching the tough, underutilized stems of asparagus in oil and infusing the oil with leeks and garlic, you get all the flavor from these woody bits and save them from the trash or the compost. Use this simple aïoli as a flavorful complement to grilled asparagus—or for poached salmon, club sandwiches, fried artichokes, French fries, or anywhere you might use mayonnaise.

YIELD: 4 SERVINGS

GRILLED ASPARAGUS:
1 bunch asparagus, with 1-2 inches
    cut off the bottom and reserved
    for aïoli
2 tablespoons olive oil

ASPARAGUS-BOTTOM AÏOLI:
1 cup olive oil

1 cup asparagus bottoms
    (from one bunch asparagus)
4 cloves garlic
1 cup leeks (light green and
    dark green parts), chopped
1 lemon, juiced
1 egg yolk
Water
Salt and pepper to taste

TO SERVE:
1 hard-boiled egg, chopped (optional)
Lemon slices (optional)

Grill the asparagus: toss the top part of the asparagus with olive oil. Heat a grill or grill pan to high heat. Grill the asparagus until tender using tongs to flip spears, about 2 minutes per side. Transfer to a plate and set aside.

Make the aïoli: in a pot, heat oil, asparagus bottoms, and garlic gently over low heat until the aparagus and garlic are soft, about 15 minutes. Stir in leek tops for the last minute (they will turn bright green). Add the lemon juice.

Transfer the mixture to a blender and puree until smooth. Strain the asparagus oil through a fine sieve, pushing through with a rubber spatula. Allow to cool. At this point you can keep the oil in the refrigerator for 3 days. Bring the mixture back to room temperature before using to make the aïoli.

To serve, whisk together the egg yolk with 1 tablespoon of water in a food processor until foamy. Slowly drizzle in the asparagus oil with the food processor running until the mayonnaise has emulsified. If it gets too thick, add a bit more water or lemon juice. Check for seasoning and serve over the grilled asparagus tops, hot or cold. Top with the chopped hard-boiled egg and serve with the lemon slices to squeeze over the asparagus, if desired.

Swiss Chard

Stem Gratin

Swiss chard stems are so versatile they can be treated like a separate vegetable. If you've already used the Swiss chard leaves for another recipe, you can make this recipe with just the stems. Caramelize some onions and add them in place of the chard leaves.

YIELD: 6 SERVINGS

1 bunch Swiss chard
1 tablespoon canola oil
1 garlic clove, minced
1 shallot, diced
15 Swiss chard leaves
2 cups cream
Salt and pepper to taste
Pinch of nutmeg
1 cup Parmesan, divided
½ cup Gruyère
1 cup homemade bread crumbs
     or panko
3 tablespoons cold butter, cubed

Preheat the oven to 350°F.

Prepare the Swiss chard: separate the Swiss chard leaves from the stems. Slice the stems into 3- to 4-inch pieces, and thinly slice the leaves into strips. Set aside the leaves.

Fill a bowl with ice water. Bring a heavy-bottomed pot of water to boil and add a pinch of salt to the water. Blanch the chard stems in the boiling water for 4 to 5 minutes, or until the stems are tender but still retain their structure. Remove and shock in a bath of ice water. After 2 minutes, remove, drain, and place on a plate lined with an absorbent kitchen towel to dry.

Make the gratin: heat a sauté pan over medium heat. Add canola oil and sweat the garlic and shallots for 3 minutes. Add the Swiss chard leaves and sauté for 1 to 2 minutes, or until wilted. Set aside.

In a heavy-bottomed pot, bring cream to a boil. Lower heat to medium and cook until cream is reduced by a third, about 5 minutes. Season with the nutmeg, salt, and pepper to taste. Add the Gruyère and ½ cup Parmesan, stirring constantly until combined. Remove from heat.

Butter the bottom of a 9 by 9-inch casserole dish and season lightly with salt. Combine the remaining Parmesan with bread crumbs. Lay the sautéed chard leaves on the bottom. Layer the Swiss chard stems on top. Pour over just enough cream to cover, making sure that the cream mixture is dispersed evenly throughout the dish. Top with the bread crumb mixture. Place the cold cubed butter on top and bake in the oven for 10 to 15 minutes, or until golden brown.

Carrot Spaetzle

Patrick Mulvaney loves to showcase tender young carrots at the height of their season in Northern California, but found that each spring he was left with a mountain of tops heading straight to the compost bin. This bright green spaetzle keeps those tops out of the compost pile, and frying the peels helps him highlight the carrot from stem to tip.

YIELD: 4 SERVINGS

CARROT TOP SPAETZLE:
1 bunch young carrots, tops removed, blanched and shocked
2 eggs
1 cup flour
½ cup milk
Salt and pepper to taste
1 teaspoon canola oil

CRISPY CARROT SKINS:
Canola oil for frying
Carrot peels from 1 bunch carrots
Rice flour
Salt and pepper to taste

TO SERVE:
1 bunch small carrots, thinly sliced into coins
3 tablespoons butter, divided
1 tablespoon spring onion, sliced
1 tablespoon spring garlic, sliced
1 to 2 ounces grated Gouda (like Cypress Grove's Midnight Moon)

Remove the tops from one bunch of young carrots and measure out one packed cup for the spaetzle dough. (The rest of the tops can be reserved for another use in the freezer, or composted.) Peel the carrots and reserve the peels for the crispy carrot skins. Slice the carrots into coins and reserve for the last step of the recipe.

Make the spaetzle dough: Puree the carrot tops and eggs in blender until smooth. Strain the mixture through a fine mesh sieve into a large bowl. Whisk in the flour until combined (the mixture will be a stiff paste). Drizzle in the milk while stirring with a wooden spoon to make a batter that should coat the back of a spoon. (You may not need all of the milk.) Add a pinch each of salt and pepper and let the dough rest on the counter for at least 20 minutes.

Make the crispy carrot skins: heat enough oil to have a depth of 2 inches in a Dutch oven over high heat until it's 350°F. Toss the washed and dried carrot peels in the rice flour. Shake off the excess and deep-fry in the hot oil until crispy. Drain on a paper towel–lined plate and season to taste with salt. Set aside until ready to serve.

Make the noodles: put a large pot of salted water over medium heat and bring to a simmer. Use a wooden spoon to press the batter through a large-holed colander directly over the simmering water. Stir gently and wait for the spaetzle to rise to the top. Do this in two or three batches to avoid crowding the pot. When the spaetzle float to the top, reserve ¼ cup cooking water. Drain the noodles, and transfer to an ice water bath to shock them and stop the cooking. Drain and transfer the spaetzle to a baking sheet. Drizzle the teaspoon of canola oil on top and toss gently to prevent the spaetzle from sticking together.

In a large sauté pan, cook the thinly cut carrot coins, garlic, and onion in 1 tablespoon butter over low heat until cooked through but not browned, about 5 minutes. Transfer vegetables to a plate and turn the heat up to medium. Add the remaining butter. When it foams, add the cooked spaetzle and toss until they're brown and toasty, about 5 minutes. Return the vegetables to the pan, add the cheese, and toss, using a bit of the cooking water to loosen the mix. Check for seasoning. Transfer everything to a serving platter, garnish with the crispy carrot skins, and serve immediately.

Carrot Pierogi

Everyone's favorite Eastern European dumpling gets a waste-saving make-over in this beta-carotene bumping recipe from chef Jamilka Borges. She juices whole carrots, using the liquid in the pierogi dough, and the pulp to round out the pork-y, spicy filling that draws flavors from Asian cuisine.

YIELD: 4 SERVINGS

5 medium carrots

DOUGH:

2 cups all-purpose flour
½ teaspoon kosher salt
½ cup reserved carrot juice
¼ cup sour cream
1 tablespoon extra-virgin olive oil
1 egg

FILLING:

2 tablespoons (about 1 slice) bacon, diced
2 tablespoons onion, minced
1½ teaspoons (about 1 large clove) garlic, minced
1½ teaspoons (about 1-inch piece) ginger, minced
½ pound ground pork
1 cup reserved carrot pulp
½ tablespoon soy sauce
1 teaspoon fish sauce
½ teaspoon sambal
1 tablespoon scallions
1½ teaspoons cilantro stems and leaves
Salt to taste
1 tablespoon lime juice

TO SERVE:

2 tablespoons butter
½ cup full-fat yogurt
¼ cup cilantro leaves

Juice the carrots using a fruit and vegetable juicer. Reserve the juice and pulp separately. Alternatively, you can blend the carrots in a high-speed blender and let the mixture sit over a fine mesh sieve to separate the juice and pulp.

Make the dough: in a stand mixer fitted with a hook attachment, combine the flour and salt on low speed. Add the remaining ingredients and mix on low until a ball of dough forms. Remove the dough from the bowl and knead by hand on a floured surface until smooth, about 5 minutes. Cover with a damp kitchen towel and let rest on the counter for 30 minutes.

Make the filling: in a big sauté pan over medium heat, cook the bacon until all the fat has rendered, about 5 minutes. Transfer bacon to a plate lined with paper towels to drain, reserving the fat in the pan. Sweat the onions and garlic in the bacon fat and cook until translucent, about 5 minutes. Add the ginger and ground pork and cook until the pork has browned, about 10 minutes. Add the carrot pulp, soy sauce, fish sauce, and sambal. Cook until the pulp has dried out, stirring frequently, about 10 minutes. Add the cilantro and scallions. Season with salt to taste and add the lime juice. Transfer to a shallow bowl or baking sheet and let the filling cool in the refrigerator for 20 minutes.

Prepare the pierogi: roll the dough out until it's ⅛-inch thick. Use a 4-inch round pastry cutter to cut the dough into circles. Place 1 tablespoon of filling on each wrapper. Fold the circle in half and pinch all the way around to seal the pierogi.

Bring a large pot of salted water to a boil. Cook the pierogi for 2 minutes and remove from the water with a slotted spoon. Heat the butter in a sauté pan over medium heat until it turns brown and smells nutty. Add the boiled pierogi and cook until they're brown and become crisp on the outside, about 5 minutes.

To serve, transfer the pierogi and any of the pan sauce to a serving platter and garnish with the yogurt and cilantro leaves.

Zhoug

Zhoug is a spicy herb sauce of Yemenite origin that you find in Syria and Israel. It's often the go-to condiment for falafel and is eaten with bread for those who want heat with every bite. It's a must with shakshuka, and you'll probably find yourself stirring it into scrambled eggs, spreading it on a sandwich, mixing it with Greek yogurt to make a dip, or just eating it by the spoonful. This recipe is adapted from an original recipe in Ana Sortun's book, *Soframiz: Vibrant Middle Eastern Recipes from Sofra Bakery and Café.*

YIELD: 1 CUP

2 Hungarian hot wax peppers, stemmed and coarsely chopped (seeds kept intact)*
2 cloves garlic, peeled
1½ cups cilantro stems and leaves (from 1 large bunch or 2 small ones)
1½ cups flat-leaf parsley stems and leaves (from 1 bunch)
½ cup extra-virgin olive oil
1½ teaspoons sherry vinegar
½ teaspoon kosher salt
1 teaspoon ground coriander
1 teaspoon ground cumin

Combine all the ingredients in a blender and blend until very, very smooth, about 2 minutes. You should have a bright green emulsified sauce. Use immediately or cover and refrigerate in an airtight container for up to 5 days.

* Sortun suggests using Hungarian hot wax peppers because they are medium spicy and have a lot of flesh, which helps give the zhoug some body and texture. If you can't find these peppers, use jalapeños instead.

Root-to-Leaf

Beet Burgers

There are countless varieties of beets, each with a particular flavor. Every part of the beet is edible from the root, to the stem, to the leaf. In these vibrant veggie burgers, Beard Award–winning chef Debbie Gold incorporates all three elements for maximum taste and minimal waste. Leftover pickled beet stems are also delicious on hamburgers, with charcuterie plates, and anywhere else you would use pickles.

YIELD: 4 BURGERS

PICKLED BEET STEMS:
Stems from 1 bunch beets
1 quart water
4 cloves garlic, peeled
3 bay leaves
¾ cup (5%) white vinegar
5 tablespoons sugar
2 tablespoons sea salt
1 teaspoon whole black peppercorns

ROASTED BEETS:
2 large beets, any color, stems reserved
    for pickling (see above)
2 sprigs thyme
2 tablespoons olive oil, divided

2 teaspoons sea salt, divided
Pepper to taste

TO SERVE:
4 hamburger buns, toasted
Roasted beets
Pickled beet stems
1 avocado, thinly sliced
4 ounces goat cheese
Fresh beet greens

Make the pickled beet stems: trim any bruised or discolored parts from the stems. Cut the stems into 2-inch pieces and place into a clean glass jar.

Combine the remaining ingredients in a large stainless steel pot. Bring to a boil. Pour the pickling liquid over the beet stems. Let the mixture cool and then place the lid on top. Shake the jar and refrigerate the stems for at least 24 hours.

Make the roasted beets: scrub the beets well to remove any dirt and trim off the leafy greens close to the top of the beet, leaving about a half inch of stem. Remove the stems from the greens and reserve both. Wash the greens and spin or pat dry.

Preheat the oven to 375°F. Tear 2 large sheets of aluminum foil. Place 1 beet on each sheet of foil. To each foil package, add 1 sprig of thyme, 1 tablespoon olive oil, and 1 teaspoon of sea salt. Wrap the beets loosely in the foil. Place the wrapped beets on a baking sheet. Roast for 50 to 60 minutes, checking for doneness every 20 minutes or so. Roast until the beets are tender. You'll know when the beets are done when a paring knife easily slides into the center of the beet.

Let the beets cool. When they're cool enough to handle, hold one of the beets in a paper towel and rub the skin away. The skin should peel away easily. Discard the thyme and foil packages. Slice the beets into ¾-inch rounds and season with salt and pepper to taste.

Build your burgers: place at least 2 slices of roasted beets on the toasted bun bottoms. Top each burger with ¼ cup pickled beet stems, ¼ of the sliced avocado, 1 ounce goat cheese, 1 to 2 leaves beet greens, and the toasted bun top. Serve immediately.

Scallops

with Carrot Top-Pistachio Pesto and Carrot Gastrique

This elegant dish delivers many layers of carrot—bottoms roasted, juice turned into a delicate gastrique, tops blended into a bright pesto—paired with seared scallops and crunchy pistachios for an exploration of the flavors and textures of the hearty root vegetable.

YIELD: 4 SERVINGS

ROASTED BABY CARROTS:
1 bunch small carrots, tops reserved
1 tablespoon thyme, chopped
1 shallot, chopped
1 clove garlic, chopped
3 tablespoons olive oil
Salt and pepper to taste

CARROT GASTRIQUE:
2 cups (about 16 fluid ounces)
    carrot juice
1 tablespoon granulated sugar
1 teaspoon kosher salt
½ cup Champagne vinegar
    or white wine vinegar

CARROT TOP-PISTACHIO PESTO:
1 bunch carrot tops, cleaned and

blanched, large stems removed
    (about 2 ounces of greens)
¼ bunch dill
½ cup toasted pistachios
⅓ cup extra-virgin olive oil
1 clove garlic
Salt and pepper to taste

SCALLOPS:
2 pounds sea scallops
    (about 20 scallops, or 5 scallops
    per entrée serving)
Salt and pepper to taste
2 tablespoons olive oil
Delicate carrot sprigs for garnish

OPTIONAL:
Scallop shells reserved for serving

Make the roasted carrots: preheat the oven to 375°F. Place all the ingredients together on a baking sheet. Mix well to ensure that the carrots are seasoned evenly. Roast the carrots in the oven for about 15 minutes, or until tender.

Make the carrot gastrique: place all the ingredients in a saucepot over medium heat. Cook until the liquid has reduced to a syruplike consistency,

about 30 minutes. Set aside until ready to serve.

Make the carrot-top pesto: in a pot of boiling water, boil carrot tops for 30 seconds. Immediately plunge in an ice bath to cool. Drain carrot tops. Put carrot tops, dill, pistachios, olive oil, garlic, salt, and pepper into a food processor and blend until smooth. Refrigerate until ready to serve. (Note: this pesto can be made a day or two in advance.)

Make the scallops: season the scallops with salt and pepper to taste. Add the oil to an ovenproof sauté pan. When the oil is smoking hot, place the scallops in the pan and cook until golden brown and cooked through, about 2 minutes, flip over and cook for 1 more minute.

To serve, place the carrot-top pesto on the shell (if using) or on a plate. Place the scallops on top of the pesto, and a few slices of roasted carrots next to the scallops. Pour the gastrique around the scallops and garnish with the carrot-top sprig.

Spaghetti

with Whole-Tomato Sauce and Artichokes

Tomatoes and artichokes are two staples of any Italian food lover's diet, yet both leave the home cook with a cutting board full of trimmings. Here, Beard Award–winning chef Sarah Grueneberg extracts flavor at every step: whole tomatoes are grated to build the sauce, tomato peels are simmered in olive oil to release extra flavor, and artichoke leaves and stems give a boost to the stock.

YIELD: 6–8 SERVINGS

ARTICHOKES AND STOCK:
8 baby artichokes or 3 globe artichokes
½ cup extra-virgin olive oil
½ cup white wine
Juice of 1 lemon
1 tablespoon kosher salt

SPAGHETTI AND SAUCE:
1 pound spaghetti or spaghettini
8 large tomatoes, preferably heirloom
    or vine-ripened (about 5 pounds)
¾ cup extra-virgin olive oil, plus more
    for drizzling
2 teaspoons kosher salt
2 cups basil, plus more for garnish
1 clove garlic, sliced thin
1 pinch chile flake
Parmesan to finish

Prepare the artichokes and stock: trim the artichokes, start by pulling off the outermost leaves until you get down to the lighter yellow leaves. Then, using a serrated knife, cut off the top third or so of the artichoke and trim the very bottom of the stem. Use a vegetable peeler to clean the stem of the artichokes. Reserve trim and leaves.

In a heavy-bottomed pot, place artichoke trimmings, 2 cups water, olive oil, wine, salt, and lemon juice and bring to a simmer.

Add cleaned artichokes to the pot and cook, uncovered, over medium heat for 20 minutes, or until tender. Remove from heat and let artichokes cool in the liquid.

Once cooled, quarter artichokes into bite-size pieces and reserve the artichoke stock for the spaghetti. (Enjoy the hearts as an appetizer or fold into the spaghetti.)

Make the tomato sauce: cut the tomatoes in half horizontally. Using a box grater, grate the tomatoes, cut-side-down over a large bowl. Reserve the peels.

Place tomato peels and ½ cup olive oil in a small saucepot over medium heat. Sweat peels in oil until tender, about 5 minutes. Season with a pinch of salt and add 4 to 5 basil leaves. Transfer peels and oil to a blender (or use an immersion blender) and blend on high until smooth and emulsified, about 1 minute. Whisk sauce into the bowl with the grated tomatoes.

In a large saucepan, heat ¾ cup olive oil over medium-high heat. Add garlic and cook until golden, about 3 minutes. Add chile flakes and tomato mixture. Bring to a boil and cook for 10 minutes, or until reduced by half. Turn off heat and reserve until ready to cook the pasta. The sauce should look thick with olive oil around the edges.

Bring a large pot of water to a boil. Season with about 3 tablespoons of kosher salt. Add spaghetti to the boiling water and cook for 6 minutes. Drain the pasta into a colander, reserving ½ cup of the pasta cooking water. The pasta will seem firm and undercooked.

Stir pasta into tomato sauce, add 1 cup of artichoke stock, and simmer slowly over low heat for 8 minutes. Add the remaining basil and artichoke hearts (if using), lower heat, and let simmer for 5 more minutes. Gradually add remaining pasta water, if needed.

Taste pasta to test doneness. It should be al dente. Finish with freshly grated cheese, basil, and a drizzle of oil.

Collard Green

Tamales

Elizabeth Falkner is obsessed with using collard greens in innovative ways like using hearty leaves as tamale wrappers, so the whole package is edible. (She even uses the stems in the tamale mix for added texture.) A drizzle of smoky mole, pecans, and chia seeds makes this one showstopping dish.

YIELD: 8 TAMALES

SMOKY PECAN-CHIA MOLE:
¼ cup dried goji berries
1 teaspoon coconut oil
½ medium onion, chopped
2 cloves garlic, minced
1 teaspoon cumin seeds
½ teaspoon ancho chile pepper
1 teaspoon chipotle powder
½ cup pecans, toasted
½ cup ground chia seeds or chia seeds
2 tablespoons sesame seeds
Salt to taste
2 ounces dark chocolate
1 tablespoon red wine vinegar
1 tablespoon tomato paste

TAMALES:
1 bunch collard greens or Swiss chard, leaves whole, stems reserved
1 tablespoon olive oil
3 teaspoons salt, divided
1 cup steel-cut oats

1 small cinnamon stick
½ cup quinoa
½ cup masa
2 teaspoons coconut oil
¼ teaspoon anise seeds
½ cup grated cotija cheese
Pepper to taste
Oil

TO SERVE:
1 cup yogurt
½ cup scallions, chopped
½ cup cilantro, chopped
2 whole limes, cut into quarters

Make the mole: in a small bowl, add goji berries and ½ cup hot water to rehydrate. Let sit for 10 minutes. In a sauté pan over medium heat, heat coconut oil. Add onions and garlic and cook for 2 minutes. Add cumin, ancho, and chipotle and cook 1 minute. Add pecans, chia seeds, sesame seeds, and a pinch of salt and sauté for 1 minute. Add rehydrated goji berries, chocolate, vinegar, tomato paste, and 3 tablespoons water. Simmer until chocolate melts. Season with salt and let cool. Transfer to a blender or food processor and puree until smooth.

Make tamale filling: in a large pot of boiling water, blanch greens for 30 seconds, then plunge in a bowl of ice water. Drain and set aside. Thinly slice the stems. Heat one tablespoon oil in a sauté pan over medium-high heat. Add stems, season with salt and pepper, and cook for 3 minutes until stems are cooked through but not mushy.

In a saucepot, add the oats and 4 cups water. Bring to a boil and add a pinch of salt and the cinnamon stick. Cook for 5 minutes. Add the quinoa and stir to combine. Cover the pot and cook for another 15 minutes, or until cooked through. Pour the oat–quinoa mixture into a large bowl and add the masa, coconut oil, anise seeds, and salt. Add the chopped stems to the mixture and let cool until room temperature. Add the cotija cheese and pepper to taste.

Make tamales: scoop 1 cup of tamale filling into a blanched leaf and roll up like a burrito: starting at one end, roll up the filling inside the leaf and then fold the sides inward while rolling. Wrap each tamale in parchment paper using the same technique.

Set in a steamer for 30 to 40 minutes, or until cooked through. Unwrap parchment and let cool.

Heat a cast-iron pan or a grill over medium heat. Drizzle oil on tamales and season with salt. Cook for 2 minutes on each side. Serve with mole, yogurt, chopped scallions, cilantro, and a wedge of lime.

Asparagus
Panna Cotta

When Morocco native Mourad Lahlou first moved to California, he was blown away by asparagus, an ingredient he'd never seen. Now he looks forward to it every spring, and loathes wasting any. To make this savory panna cotta, he reserves the woody bottoms for stock, purees the trimmings for the custard, and highlights the blanched spears with tangy sumac and preserved lemon.

YIELD: 4 SERVINGS

1½ pounds thick asparagus spears
¼ cup plus 2 tablespoons whole milk
1 packet gelatin (2¼ teaspoons)
½ cup plus 2 tablespoons heavy cream
Kosher salt
1 tablespoon sumac
1 tablespoon extra-virgin olive oil
1 teaspoon lemon juice
½ preserved lemon, store bought or
    homemade (recipe on page 190)
4 poached eggs, warm
1 teaspoon flat-leaf parsley, chopped

Make panna cotta: bring a large pot of salted water to a boil. Fill a medium bowl with ice water. Trim asparagus to 4 inches. Reserve trimmings, cutting off the white, woody end pieces.

Blanch asparagus tops in boiling water until tender, about 2½ minutes. Immediately plunge them in ice water and let cool. Remove tops from ice water and drain on paper towels. Refrigerate the 12 nicest tops for garnish. Reserve the rest for the puree.

Meanwhile, blanch the trimmings in the boiling water until very soft (since they will be pureed), about 5 minutes. Immediately plunge the trimmings in the ice water and let cool completely. Remove from the ice water and drain on paper towels. Coarsely chop the trimmings. You will need 1½ cups. If there is not enough, use a few of the reserved spears for the puree.

Pour the milk into a medium saucepan and sprinkle the gelatin evenly over the top. Whisk until there are no lumps. Let the gelatin soften (or bloom) in the cold milk for 5 minutes. Stir in the cream. Set the pan over low heat, stirring gently, but continuously, to dissolve the gelatin. The mixture should always be just warm to the touch, but not hot. Continue stirring until the gelatin dissolves, about 3 minutes. Set aside to cool slightly.

Choose 4 serving bowls with a capacity of about ½ cup each.

Put the 1½ cups of trimmings in a high-powered blender with 1 tablespoon of ice water and blend until completely smooth. It might be necessary to periodically stop the blender, scrape down the sides, and redistribute the asparagus to get the blades to catch and blend completely.

Strain the cream mixture through a fine mesh strainer into the blender and pulse to combine, scraping down the sides as needed to evenly incorporate. Season to taste with salt. Strain the puree into a large liquid measuring cup. Divide the puree among the bowls, let cool to room temperature, then refrigerate overnight.

To serve, spread the sumac on a small plate or saucer. In a separate bowl, combine the olive oil, lemon juice, and a pinch of salt. Dip the bottom ½ inch of each chilled asparagus spear into the vinaigrette, letting any excess run off, and then dip one side in the sumac, tapping off any excess. Transfer to a plate.

Poach eggs: bring a shallow pan of water to a boil and lower the heat to a very slow simmer. Crack an egg into a cup and gently slide the egg into the simmering water. Add the 3 other eggs using the same method, gently pushing them apart from one another with a slotted spoon. Turn off the heat, cover pan and set timer to 4 minutes. Remove eggs with a slotted spoon.

Cut the peel away from the flesh of the preserved lemon, trim off any pith, and thinly slice the peel.

Serve panna cotta in the bowls, or remove them by running a little hot water over bottom of the bowls to loosen them. With a butter knife, carefully run blade around the edge of the panna cotta and invert onto a plate.

Set each poached egg on the top of each panna cotta and sprinkle with a very small pinch of sumac. Lay the dipped spears next to the eggs, sprinkle with the parsley, and garnish with the thinly sliced preserved lemon.

Whole Orange

Almond Cake

Our namesake hated seeing good food go to waste. True to form, his flourless orange and almond cake uses every bit of the citrus, pureeing them whole to extract all the flavor and oils from the peels and spinning them into this vibrant, virtually effortless dessert. By not stopping short of pureeing the oranges too fine, you wind up with little bits of skin, which will not be at all bitter after the long boiling and very pleasant to bite on. A tip from Beard himself: it will not rise very much, and you may wonder if it will ever bake firm. Don't worry, it will.

YIELD: 8 SERVINGS

2 large oranges
　　(preferably seedless navels)
6 eggs
1½ cups ground almonds
Pinch of salt
1 cup sugar
1 teaspoon baking powder

GARNISH:
Thin slices of peeled orange
　　sprinkled with confectioners'
　　sugar and a touch of cinnamon,
　　or fresh raspberries
Whipped cream

Preheat oven to 400°F. Butter and flour a deep 9-inch cake pan.

Bring a large pot of salted water to a boil. Wash the oranges and place them in the boiling water; cover the pot. Boil until very soft, about 30 minutes. Drain, cool, cut into quarters, removing any seeds.

Process the oranges to a fairly fine puree in a blender or food processor, or put them through a meat grinder.

Beat the eggs in a bowl until thick then add the ground almonds, salt, sugar, baking powder, and orange puree. Mix well.

Pour into cake pan and bake for 1 hour, or until the cake is firm to the touch when pressed with the tip of your finger.

Remove the pan to a rack and allow the cake to cool. Turn it out of the pan into a serving dish. Serve garnished with orange slices or berries and whipped cream.

Chocolate–Avocado Pudding

Unlike money, avocados do grow on trees—but they still cost a pretty penny, which means there's nothing worse than seeing beloved "butter fruit" over-ripened until its bruised and browned. But don't say adios to those avocados yet! Jamie Simpson transforms guacamole rejects into a decadent, creamy, yet also dairy-free and healthier version of the pudding snack packs of our youth.

YIELD: 4 SERVINGS

2 bruised avocados, cored and diced
½ cup agave, or more to taste
    (preferably organic blue agave)
3 tablespoons high quality cocoa
    powder
½ teaspoon kosher salt
Sliced strawberries, toasted and
    chopped pistachios or hazelnuts,
    and extra-virgin olive oil for
    serving (optional)

Make the chocolate-avocado pudding: in a blender, combine first four ingredients until smooth. Use a rubber spatula to scrape down the sides of the blender and repeat. Taste and add a little more agave if you'd like it sweeter. Transfer to the refrigerator and chill for 2 to 3 hours.

To serve, scoop the chilled pudding into serving bowls or cups. If you like, top with strawberries, toasted pistachios or hazelnuts, and olive oil.

2.

Meat, Bones, Skin & Scales

1   Buy meat, poultry, and fish on the bone.
     Save the bones for making stocks,
     or cook larger meat bones (not fish
     or poultry) and feed them to pets.

2   Chefs often buy fish whole and on the
     bone because the bone imparts flavor.
     The meat from fish heads is also
     incredibly flavorful.

3   If you'd rather not butcher fish at home,
     ask your fishmonger to save the fish
     collars for you. They would most likely
     be ecstatic to sell what is typically
     a food waste item.

4   After removing the filets from fish, the
     bones can be scraped with a teaspoon
     to produce piles of delicious meat
     that can be used for salads, sausages,
     soups, risottos, and so much more,
     while the bones are used to make
     stock for broth, soups, risottos, stews,
     and the like.

5   After you cook meat on the bone, roast all of the solid bits and bones and use to make more richly flavored stocks for sauces and soups.

6   Save bacon grease, ham drippings, and schmaltz in a glass jar in the refrigerator to use in other dishes that call for oil or fat. The "gumbo" of flavors in the jar will become part of your house flavor, making your cooking unique to your kitchen.

Whole Jerk Fish

While jerk chicken holds a special place in Tiffany Derry's heart, she turns to this recipe when craving something a little different. Derry advises treating this dish like an edible choose-your-own-adventure story: start with a whole fish (you'll get more flavor from the bones than just working with fillets), skip the traditional dried herbs for fresh (they'll season quickly without overpowering the fish), and from there, the world is your oyster (or rather, your redfish or snapper, in this case). As Derry says, "The beautiful thing about jerk recipes is that every household will have a different version."

YIELD: 4 SERVINGS

FOR THE FISH:
1 (3-pound) redfish or red snapper
Salt and pepper to taste

JERK MARINADE:
½ cup cilantro, roughly chopped
½ cup parsley, roughly chopped
¼ cup packed basil
¼ cup green onion, chopped
2 limes, one juiced, one cut into wedges
1 Scotch bonnet or habanero pepper
A few sprigs of mint
2 tablespoons ginger, peeled and grated
2 tablespoons soy sauce
2 cloves garlic
1 tablespoon allspice
1 teaspoon ground cumin
1 teaspoon paprika
2 pinches nutmeg
Olive oil to taste

Preheat the oven to 425°F. Score the fish down to the bone so that the jerk seasoning will flavor all the way through. Season the fish lightly with salt and pepper.

Make the jerk marinade: in a mortar and pestle or food processor, combine all of the marinade ingredients except for the olive oil. Pulse a few times to make a paste. Rub the jerk marinade all over the fish. Allow to sit for 10 to 15 minutes. Do not marinade for over 1 hour.

Make the whole jerk fish: in a large baking dish or rimmed baking sheet, lay the fish on its side and cook until lightly charred and cooked through, about 20 minutes. Serve with lime wedges and a drizzle of olive oil.

Fisherman's Stew

This efficient recipe from Mike Isabella uses shrimp shells, fish heads, and bones as the flavorful foundation for kakavia, a Greek stew, which also highlights underutilized cuts, like fish cheeks and collars.

YIELD: 4 SERVINGS

FISH STOCK:
2 tablespoons canola oil
Bones from a 2- to 4-pound white fish
    (such as snapper or striped bass)
6 ounces shrimp shells (25 to 30 shrimp)
4 cloves garlic, smashed
2 stalks celery, chopped
1 medium carrot, chopped
1 head fennel, chopped
1 Spanish onion, chopped
2 tablespoons tomato paste
1 cup white wine
10 sprigs thyme
2 bay leaves
1 teaspoon whole black peppercorns
1 gallon water

KAKAVIA SAUCE (4 CUPS):
½ cup shaved shallots
2 tablespoons shaved garlic
2 tablespoons extra-virgin olive oil
5 cups tomato juice
2 cups homemade fish stock

ROASTED FISH HEADS:
2 fish heads from 2 white fish
2 tablespoons extra-virgin olive oil
Salt to taste
6 sprigs thyme
4 cloves garlic, smashed
2 bay leaves
Peel from 1 lemon

STEW:
2 tablespoons canola oil
10 shrimp, peeled and deveined
15 cockles
15 Prince Edward Island mussels
1 cup white wine
½ teaspoon Aleppo pepper
Salt and fresh ground pepper, to taste
3½ cups kakavia sauce
1 tablespoon butter
Meat from roasted fish heads
1 tablespoon parsley, chopped
1 tablespoon dill, chopped
Toasted bread for serving

Make fish stock: add oil to a large, heavy-bottomed pot and heat until it shimmers. Sear fish bones and shrimp shells until nicely browned, about 5 minutes. Remove bones and shells and set aside. Add vegetables and cook on medium for 5 minutes. Add tomato paste and cook for 5 minutes. Stir constantly to prevent scorching. Add wine, thyme, bay leaves, and peppercorns and cook until liquid has reduced by half, about 10 minutes. Add water, bring stock to a simmer, then cook for 45 minutes, skimming off impurities that float to the surface. Strain through a fine mesh sieve and set aside.

Make kakavia sauce: add shallots, garlic, and oil to a cold pot and heat slowly over medium-low heat. This will prevent browning and keep the oil from losing its flavor. Cook garlic and shallots until tender, about 10 minutes. Add tomato juice and fish stock to pot and bring to a simmer.

Cook for 1½ to 2 hours, or until the liquid has reduced by half, making sure to skim off any oil or fat that floats to the surface. Scrape the sides of the pot with a rubber spatula during this process to prevent the sides from burning. Remove from heat and set aside.

Make the roasted fish heads: preheat the oven to 300°F. Coat the fish heads generously with the olive oil and salt to taste. Make a bed using the herbs, garlic, bay leaves, and lemon peel on a baking sheet and place the fish heads on top. Roast in the oven for 30 to 60 minutes, or until you can easily pull the bones from the meat.

Remove fish heads from oven and let cool for 10 minutes. While warm, pick the meat from the bones. (Don't forget about the cheeks!) Be careful that there are no small bones or skin in the meat, and try keep it in large pieces.

Make stew: add oil to a heavy-bottomed pot over medium-high heat. When oil is hot, add shrimp and sear on one side for 2 minutes. Remove shrimp and set aside. Add cockles and mussels and sauté until they start to pop open, about 1 minute. Add wine and Aleppo pepper and season with salt and black pepper. Cover and cook until wine has reduced by half, about 4 minutes.

Return shrimp to pot and add the kakavia sauce and butter. Simmer until sauce has emulsified and mussels and clams finish opening, about 3 minutes.

When shrimp are cooked through and mussels and cockles are fully open, add picked fish head meat and lower heat to warm, stirring gently. Check seasonings and finish with chopped herbs. Serve with toasted bread.

Tahini–Pomegranate
Snapper Collars

Collars are a little-known fish butchering gem deserving of some time in the sun. Anchored by the collarbone, this cut runs from top to bottom behind the clavicle, and features rich meat near the belly, ending in a fat cap. Score some at an Asian-market fish counter, or see if your local fishmonger has some hiding in the back.

YIELD: 4 TO 6 SERVINGS

½ cup olive oil, divided
1 shallot, finely diced
1 clove garlic, thinly sliced
1 Fresno chile, sliced
Leaves from 4 sprigs thyme
Leaves from 1 sprig oregano
5 tablespoons pomegranate molasses
3 tablespoons lemon juice
2 tablespoons tahini paste
3 collars from 3 large snappers
1 cup Greek yogurt
Salt and pepper to taste

Make the tahini-pomegranate glaze: heat 1 tablespoon oil in a saucepan over medium heat. Add the shallots, garlic, Fresno chile, thyme, and oregano and cook until the onion is translucent. Whisk in the pomegranate molasses, lemon juice, and tahini. Lower the heat and cook the mixture until it has reduced to a thickened glaze, about 3 minutes. Season with salt and pepper. (Note: the glaze will continue to thicken after taken off the heat.

If needed, add a bit of water to keep it viscous.)

Prepare the snapper collars: preheat a grill or broiler to medium heat. Rinse and dry the fish collars. In a bowl, toss the collars with the Greek yogurt and season with salt and pepper to taste. Brush the collars with 2 tablespoons olive oil. Cook over indirect heat until the bones are loose and the collar has cooked through, about 5 minutes. Baste with the glaze throughout the cooking process.

Once the meat easily pulls away from the bone, remove the collars from the grill or broiler. Brush on a final coating of the glaze and serve.

Crispy Grouper Collars

While collars are great broiled or grilled, their meaty texture also holds up exceptionally well to frying, as in this recipe for tempura-fried collars with notes of cool, spicy, and sweet. William Dissen describes how to remove collars if butchering at home, but if you're short on time, do your local fishmonger a favor by buying an item that usually goes to waste.

YIELD: 4 SERVINGS

SWEET CHILE SAUCE:
¾ cup wildflower honey
1 tablespoon plus 1 teaspoon garlic-
    chile sauce (such as sambal olek)
1 tablespoon rice wine vinegar
1½ teaspoons lime juice
1 clove garlic, minced
1 (¼-inch) piece ginger, minced
¼ teaspoon lemongrass, minced
¼ teaspoon cilantro, finely chopped
¼ teaspoon mint, finely chopped
Salt and ground black pepper to taste

GREEN GARLIC AÏOLI:
1 head green garlic (or 3 cloves garlic)
1 cup mayonnaise
1 tablespoon lemon juice
Salt and ground black pepper to taste

KOHLRABI-FRESNO CHILE SLAW:
1 kohlrabi, peeled and julienned
½ cup julienned fennel
¼ cup olive oil
¼ cup julienned red onion
¼ cup julienned red bell pepper
1 Fresno chile pepper, cut into rings
2 tablespoons basil, chiffonade
2 tablespoons cider vinegar
1 teaspoon honey
Salt and ground black pepper to taste

GROUPER:
½ cup all-purpose flour
½ cup cornstarch
1 cup soda water
Salt and ground black pepper to taste
2 whole grouper, scaled and gutted
    (or 2 collars)
6 cups vegetable oil for frying
1 tablespoon ground Aleppo pepper

Make chile sauce: in a bowl, mix all ingredients until combined. Season with salt and pepper. Refrigerate.

Make aïoli: bring a pot of water to a simmer and blanch garlic until tender, about 4 minutes. Shock in a bowl of ice water. Drain and transfer to a blender. Puree until smooth, about 1 minute. You should end up with about ¼ cup. Whisk mayonnaise, garlic puree, and lemon juice. Season with salt and pepper. Refrigerate.

Make slaw: place all ingredients into a bowl and toss. Season with salt and pepper and refrigerate. (This can be done up to 1 hour before serving.)

Make tempura batter: in a large bowl, combine flour and cornstarch and whisk in soda water—the batter should be thin. Season with salt and pepper. Refrigerate.

If using whole fish, butcher the grouper by removing the fillets from the head and spine. Reserve the grouper fillets for another recipe. Remove the collars from the neck and head of the fish by inserting a knife behind the gills and carefully filleting the neck away from the head of the fish, removing the tender underside of the neck. After removing the neck (or collar), use your knife to remove any pin bones. The pectoral fin of the grouper will still remain intact along the exterior of the collar. The collars are now ready to be cooked.

In a Dutch oven, heat oil to 350°F. Dip collars into batter and gently tap against the side of the bowl to remove excess batter. Place collars into the oil and cook for about 4 minutes, or until the batter is set and golden and fish is cooked through. Remove collars from fryer and drain on a paper towel-lined plate to remove any excess oil. Season to taste with salt and pepper.

To serve, place a large round circle of the green garlic aïoli on 4 plates. Place a grouper collar and ¼ of the kohlrabi slaw on each plate.

Sprinkle with dried Aleppo pepper around the plate, dollop sweet chile sauce on the side, and serve immediately.

Aku Scraping Tartare

In Mark Noguchi's native Hawaii, deep-fried aku (or ahi) bones are popular among locals. When you butcher aku (or any raw sashimi-grade fish), there is enough meat on the bone to be scraped with a spoon and served raw. Here he shares his take on the raw preparation, which is served atop crispy tempura-fried nori seaweed. If you have any smoked macadamia nuts left over, they can be used in salads, on eggs, over soups, or anywhere you want to add some smoky crunch.

YIELD: 4 TO 6 SERVINGS

SMOKED MACADAMIA NUTS:
1 cup macadamia nuts
1 teaspoon Hawaiian salt
1 small Hawaiian or Thai chile pepper, roughly chopped
½ cup wood chips, soaked in water

AKU SCRAPING:
1 pound bone scrapings from aku, ahi, or any raw sashimi-grade fish
1 small sweet onion, sliced paper thin
1 Hawaiian or Thai bird chile, minced
1 tablespoon smoked macadamia nuts
1 teaspoon minced ginger
1 teaspoon soy sauce
¼ teaspoon konbu dashi

TEMPURA NORI:
1 box tempura mix

16 small sheets nori (2 × 4 inches)
Kosher salt

TO SERVE:
3 green onions, cut into 2-inch sections and then lengthwise into thin threads
1 teaspoon rice bran or sesame oil
Hawaiian salt to garnish

Combine the macadamia nuts, salt, and chile pepper in a large bowl. Set in a metal steamer or colander that fits inside of a large pot or wok. Line with lots of foil. Place the wood chips in the bottom. Light a corner of the wood chips with a lighter. Place a round cooling rack over the wood chips so that it is raised up and not touching the chips. Then, place the colander or steamer with the macadamia nut mixture on top of that. Seal the entire thing with more foil. Keep over medium-low heat so that the chips are smoking constantly. Be sure to have the hood fan running. Keep smoking until the nuts are a deep brown color, approximately 45 minutes. Check at 30 minutes. (Alternatively, heat the oven to 400°F. Transfer the plain nuts to a baking sheet and roast until they are a deep brown color, about 10 minutes. Remove from oven and immediately toss with the salt and chile pepper.)

Let the nuts cool and pulse in a food processor until they're chopped into ¼-inch pieces. Store in an airtight container. This will keep for 1 month, but can be extended to 2 to 3 months by freezing.

Make the aku scraping: in a large bowl, gently fold the aku, onion, chile pepper, macadamia nuts, ginger, shoyu, and dashi together. Taste and check for seasonings. Set aside.

Make the tempura nori: in a large heavy pot or Dutch oven, heat the oil to 350°F.

Prepare the tempura mix according to the instructions on box. Be sure that you have at least 1 cup of batter. Working in batches, lightly dredge the nori through the batter. Immediately drop nori into the oil, making sure to hold the nori by two corners to keep a flat shape. Fry until batter crisps up, about 2 minutes per side. Remove nori to a paper towel–lined plate and season with kosher salt. Set aside.

To serve, take 2 tablespoons of the aku fish scrapings and spread it gently onto the tempura nori. You want to keep the nori fluffy, so do not press it down. Garnish with a drizzle of the rice bran oil, the green onion threads, and Hawaiian salt. Serve immediately.

Striped Bass Fritters

Here's another method for transforming leftover fish bones into a meal. Matt McClure's technique for roasting fish carcasses arose so he could take full advantage of the sustainably harvested fish he has to have flown into landlocked Arkansas, but this approach works regardless of your proximity to the shore and it yields not one, but two dishes. Roasting loosens the meat and makes it easier to remove for whipping up these light fritters, and leaves behind flavorful bones perfect for making a rich fish stock. If you have any remaining batter, drop small spoonfuls into the fryer to make hushpuppies.

YIELD: 15 TO 18 FRITTERS

ROASTED FISH CARCASS:
1 whole striped bass, fillets removed
½ teaspoon canola or blended oil
    (1 part extra-virgin olive oil with
    2 parts canola) per 1 pound of fish

FRITTERS:
1 cup mayonnaise
1 stalk celery, diced
1 medium-size shallot, diced small
½ cup panko bread crumbs
2 tablespoons hot sauce
1 tablespoon lemon juice
1 tablespoon kosher salt
1 tablespoon parsley, chopped
Picked striped bass meat (about 2 cups)
10 cups vegetable oil for frying

TEMPURA BATTER:
2 cups all-purpose flour
1 cup white wine
1 tablespoon baking powder
1 teaspoon kosher salt
2 cups soda water

TO SERVE:
1 cup crème fraîche
2 tablespoons dill, chopped
1 tablespoon plus 1 teaspoon
    lemon juice, divided
½ head of fennel, shaved thin
10 celery leaves

Roast the fish: Preheat the oven to 350°F. Lightly oil the fish carcass and place on a foil-lined baking sheet. Roast in the oven for about 7 minutes, just until the meat can be easily flaked away from the bones using a fork. Let cool for 10 minutes. Pick the meat from the bones, collar, and cheeks and set aside. (Note: reserve bones for stock.)

Make the fritters: in a large mixing bowl, use a wooden spoon or rubber spatula to mix together mayonnaise, celery, shallots, bread crumbs, hot sauce, lemon juice, salt, and parsley. Gently fold in the picked bass meat until just incorporated. Try to leave the fish in as big of pieces as possible. Scoop the mixture into 2-inch balls and place on a baking sheet. Refrigerate until ready to fry.

Make the tempura batter: in a large bowl, mix together the dry ingredients. Whisk in the wine, then add the soda water until you reach a consistency slightly thinner than pancake batter. Refrigerate until ready to fry.

In a large heavy-bottomed pot or Dutch oven, heat the vegetable oil to 350°F. Working in batches, use a fork to dip the pre-rolled fish balls into the tempura batter, allowing the batter to fully coat the fish. Gently place the coated fish balls into the hot oil. Use a metal slotted spoon to move the balls in the oil a bit so that they do not stick. Fry for 2 to 3 minutes, or until golden brown. Remove fritters from the fryer and place on a paper towel–lined plate.

In a small mixing bowl, toss the shaved fennel with 1 teaspoon lemon juice. In another small mixing bowl, mix together the crème fraîche, dill, and 1 tablespoon lemon juice.

Place fritters on a plate, garnish with fennel and celery leaves and serve with crème fraîche sauce on the side.

Grilled Swordfish Skin

with Grapefruit and Rainbow Swiss Chard Stems

For many people, the best part of a fish is the crispy skin. Amy Brandwein dispenses with pretense entirely to make the fish skin the star of the show in this crunchy, citrusy appetizer. Brandwein advises that this is a great use of any skin you have left over from other swordfish preparations, but you can also help reduce food waste on the retail level by asking your local fishmonger if they'll sell you any swordfish skin that would otherwise be heading for the trash. Try this recipe with salmon skin, too. This recipe also makes use of the colorful stems of rainbow Swiss chard; the next time you are sautéing the green leaves, save the stems for this recipe.

YIELD: 4 APPETIZER SERVINGS

1 (6×6-inch) piece swordfish skin, from a 5-pound piece of swordfish (ask your fishmonger since it's often discarded when fish are cleaned for market)

Stems from 4 leaves of rainbow Swiss chard

Salt and pepper to taste

¼ tablespoon extra-virgin olive oil

1 grapefruit, skin and pith removed

¼ lemon

12 pieces micro-shiso and pea shoots (about ¼ cup)

12 leaves African blue basil or regular basil

Prepare the fish skin: using a sharp knife, cut the swordfish skin into rectangles, approximately 2 × 6 inches each. Set aside.

Make the rainbow Swiss chard: bring a small pot of water to a boil and season with salt. Boil the chard stems until tender, about 2 minutes, and place in an ice water bath. Remove the stems after they've chilled, about 5 minutes. Let the stems dry on a dishtowel-lined plate. Cut the stems into matchstick-size pieces. Place in a small bowl, season with salt and pepper, and dress with 1 tablespoon extra-virgin olive oil.

Cut the peeled grapefruit in half. Slice into very thin pieces and set aside.

Grill the swordfish skin: season the swordfish skin pieces with salt and pepper and drizzle with olive oil. Heat a grill to medium heat. Cook the swordfish skin approximately 1 to 2 minutes on both sides until crisp. Alternatively, cook the skin in a hot sauté pan over medium heat.

Place the grapefruit slices on a serving plate. Add grilled swordfish skin top, alternating with the Swiss chard stems. Squeeze a little fresh lemon juice on top and drizzle with some olive oil. Finish with the shiso and basil.

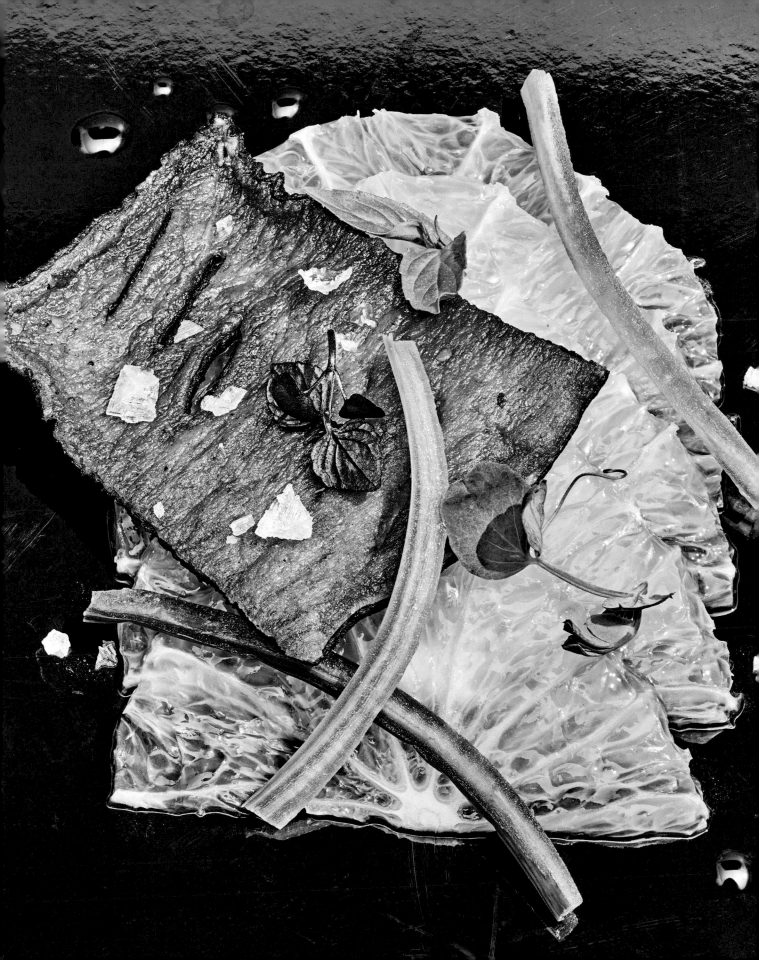

Whey-Cooked Heirloom Grains

Nothing beats homemade ricotta or Greek yogurt, but what is the homesteader hobbyist to do with all the whey? You could throw this protein-packed leftover into a smoothie, but for a more savory application, consider this recipe from William Dissen. Just as using broth or stock in place of water amps up the flavor of grains, whey gives them an extra nutritional and gustatory boost.

YIELD: 4 SERVINGS

1 tablespoon olive oil
1 medium onion, minced
2 cloves garlic, minced
2 cups water
2 cups whey
1 cup Anson Mills Yellow Stone Ground Grits (or any other grain)
½ cup heavy cream
1 tablespoon hot sauce (or to taste)
Salt and pepper to taste

In a medium pot, heat the oil over medium heat. Add the onions and cook until tender, about 4 minutes. Stir in the garlic and cook until aromatic, about 30 seconds more. Stir in the water and whey and bring to a boil over high heat.

In a steady stream, whisk in the grits and stir vigorously. Bring to a simmer, stirring constantly. When the grits begin to simmer and bubble, turn off the heat and cover the pot with a tight-fitting lid. Keep in a warm place for 1 hour to allow to steam.

Remove the cover and bring the grits back to a simmer over medium heat. Add the heavy cream and stir vigorously, working the sides of the pot to prevent burning. Finish with the hot sauce, salt, and pepper. Adjust the seasoning as necessary. Keep hot and serve immediately, or allow to cool and keep in the refrigerator until needed. Reheat with more whey, as needed.

Herb-Roasted Chicken

with

Charred Broccoli

Seamus Mullen takes the concept of waste reduction to a whole new level with this series of recipes that yields not one, not two, but three separate meals. First up, a roast chicken doused in an herbaceous marinade and served with impressive whole-charred broccoli heads. Leftovers become the base for a superior chicken salad (the recipe for which appears on page 73), and the chicken bones are used in a consommé (page 74) that works on its own, or as the foundation for a light, restorative soup. In fact, this recipe is so rewarding that Mullen recommends roasting an extra chicken to make sure there's enough leftover meat to go around.

YIELD: 4 SERVINGS

MARINADE:
1 cup extra-virgin olive oil
4 cloves garlic
Zest of 1 lemon
1 tablespoon chopped parsley
1 tablespoon chopped sage
1 tablespoon chopped thyme

CHICKEN:
1 (2–3 pound) whole pastured chicken
1 tablespoon ground sumac
Sea salt and freshly ground pepper
   to taste

CHARRED BROCCOLI:
4 tablespoons olive oil
2 large heads of broccoli, left whole
   and stems removed and set aside
   for pickling (see page 73)
Chile flakes
Sea salt

Preheat the oven to 375°F.

Make the marinade: in a food processor, combine the olive oil with the garlic, lemon zest, parsley, sage, and thyme and blitz until fully incorporated.

Prepare the chicken: in a glass or enamel roasting pan large enough to fit the entire chicken, smear the chicken with half of the olive oil mixture and season generously with sumac, sea salt, and pepper. Using butcher's twine, truss the legs together and wings behind the back. Place the bird, breast-side up, and roast in the oven until the meat reads 155°F at the joint with a meat thermometer, about 35 to 45 minutes, depending upon the size of the bird.

Prepare the broccoli: in a large cast-iron pan, heat 4 tablespoons olive oil over medium-high heat. Rub the heads of broccoli with the remaining olive oil–herb marinade, then season with chile flakes and salt to taste.

Using kitchen tongs and working with one head of broccoli at a time, cook the broccoli, turning until evenly charred all over. Repeat with the other head of broccoli. Turn off the heat, remove the broccoli from the pan, and cut into quarters. The broccoli should still be raw inside. Return quartered broccoli to the pan or transfer to a sheet pan if you need more space, place the pan in the oven above the chicken, and roast until broccoli is cooked through and tender, about 15 to 20 minutes.

Once chicken is cooked through, remove from oven and set aside for 5 to 10 minutes before carving. Serve with charred broccoli.

Chicken Salad

with
Pickled Broccoli Stems
and Salsa Verde

This ain't your mother's chicken salad. Seamus Mullen takes the tough stems from his charred broccoli (see page 70), and pickles them to add an acidic punch. The dish is completed with the leftover meat and herbs from his whole-roasted chicken recipe, for a salad that is bright, crunchy, and dressed in an addictive salsa verde.

YIELD: 2 SERVINGS

PICKLED BROCCOLI STEMS:
⅔ cup cider vinegar
⅓ cup water
1 tablespoon honey
Stems from 2 to 3 heads of
    broccoli, peeled

SALSA VERDE:
1 cup leftover herbs, chopped
1 cup extra-virgin olive oil
Juice and zest of 2 lemons
1 clove garlic, grated on a Microplane
1 shallot, finely minced
1 teaspoon chile flakes

SALAD:
2 cups pulled leftover chicken meat
1 cup Tuscan kale, minced
1 cup pickled broccoli stems,
    cut into ¼-inch brunoise
2 stalks celery, cut into ¼-inch
    thick pieces
1 carrot, cut into ¼-inch pieces
1 cucumber, diced
¼ cup walnuts, chopped
Sea salt and freshly ground black
    pepper
1 cup salsa verde

Pickle the broccoli stems: combine the vinegar, water, and honey in a medium saucepot and bring to a boil. Turn off heat, add broccoli stems, and allow them to cool in the liquid. They can be used after 20 minutes or you can leave them in the liquid overnight.

Make the salsa verde: combine the herbs, olive oil, lemon juice, lemon zest, garlic, shallot, and chile flakes in a bowl and mix thoroughly.

In a separate bowl, combine the pulled chicken, kale, broccoli stems, celery, carrots, cucumbers, and walnuts. Season to taste with salt and pepper. Add the salsa verde and toss to combine before serving.

Gingered Chicken Consommé

The final piece of Seamus Mullen's chicken trifecta is this delicate, ginger-spiked stock, which uses the bones from his herb-roasted chicken. Mullen often sips the broth on its own, but it can easily be served as a light soup with sliced fresh shiitake mushrooms and some green vegetables, such as okra or mustard greens, just barely poached in broth.

YIELD: 4 QUARTS

2 chicken carcasses
2 large carrots, cut in 2-inch chunks
2 stalks celery, cut in 2-inch chunks
2 large pieces dried konbu seaweed
2 bay leaves
1 cup dried shiitake mushrooms
1 head garlic
1 large knob ginger
1 large onion, quartered
Salt and pepper to taste

TO SERVE:
3 tablespoons freshly grated ginger
Chopped cilantro
Cider vinegar to taste
Fresh lime juice

In a large pot, combine the chicken carcasses, carrots, celery, konbu, bay leaves, mushrooms, garlic, ginger, onion, salt, and pepper. Cover with water and place over medium-high heat. Bring to a boil, lower the heat, and simmer for 3 to 4 hours. Remove from the heat and strain through a fine mesh sieve, discarding all the solids. If you want a clearer broth, pour through a cheesecloth or in small batches through a paper coffee filter fitted to a glass pour-over coffee maker.

Finish with the ginger and chopped cilantro. Season with salt, pepper, the cider vinegar, and a squeeze of lime juice.

Pork Cheek Sugo

with
Fava Leaf Green Noodles

Zazu kitchen + farm chef Duskie Estes is known for her passionate advocacy of sustainable meat, a philosophy she puts into action by utilizing every part of the animals that appear on her menu. This versatile recipe can be made with pork cheeks, a whole pig's head, or pork shoulder, depending on your access to lesser-known cuts. (Estes recommends visiting your local specialty butcher store for more variety.) The green noodles are made with the abundant leaves from a fava bean plant, which Estes also incorporates into salads and pestos when she has them left over from fava dishes. You can sub in spinach or arugula if needed.

YIELD: 8 TO 10 SERVINGS

PORK CHEEK SUGO:
2½ pounds pork cheeks, cleaned
Kosher salt and freshly ground black
      pepper to taste
2 tablespoons olive oil
4 medium carrots, peeled and diced
9 celery ribs, diced
2 medium yellow onions, diced
4 garlic cloves, peeled and smashed
¼ teaspoon chile flakes
1⅓ cups red wine
3 (28 ounce) cans tomatoes

2½ cups chicken stock
¼ bunch oregano, picked and
      roughly chopped
2 Calabrian chiles (or Serrano chiles)
1 bay leaf
½ cup unsalted butter
Kosher salt and freshly ground
      black pepper to taste

GREEN NOODLES:
10 ounces (about 10 cups) fava leaves
      (or arugula or spinach)
7 medium eggs
½ teaspoon kosher salt
5 cups all-purpose flour, plus more
      as needed for rolling

TO SERVE:
1 stick butter
Green noodles
Pork cheek sugo
Quality extra-virgin olive oil
Grated Parmesan cheese

Preheat the oven to 350°F.
    Prepare the pork: season the pork cheeks generously with salt and pepper. In a large Dutch oven, sear the meat in the olive oil over high heat until browned on all sides. Set aside. Brown the carrots, celery, onion, garlic, and chile flakes in the same pan, stirring to scrape up any brown bits. Add the

pork cheeks back in and add the wine; let simmer for 5 minutes. Add the tomatoes, stock, oregano, chiles, and bay leaf. Cover with foil and roast in the oven until the meat is very tender, about 3 hours. Remove bay leaf and chiles from pot; discard. Remove the meat and transfer to a large bowl. Using two forks, gently shred the meat and then return to the pot.
    Make the pasta: while meat cooks, process the fava leaves with the eggs and salt in a food processor. In a large bowl, add the "green eggs" into the center of the flour and incorporate with a wooden spoon. Transfer to a work surface and knead until smooth, about 8 minutes. Cover with plastic wrap and let sit at room temperature for 1 hour.
    Unwrap and quarter dough; cover all but one piece with plastic wrap. Using your hands, flatten the piece of dough into a rectangle. Pass the dough through the widest setting of a hand-cranked pasta roller. Fold dough into thirds to create another rectangle; pass the dough through the widest setting again, feeding open edge first; repeat folding and rolling twice. Decrease setting one notch; roll pasta through to make a thinner pasta sheet. Lower setting again; repeat through each setting until thin. Transfer the

pasta sheet to a floured work surface; repeat above steps with remaining dough pieces. With a knife or pizza cutter, cut rolled sheets of pasta into wide pappardelle noodles.

Heat a large pot of water until boiling. Season with lots of salt. Cook the noodles for 2 minutes or until al dente. Drain the noodles and rinse with cold water to stop the cooking.

For each serving, heat 1½ cups sugo in a saucepan, then toss with 1 cup cooked pasta. Remove from the heat and add 1 tablespoon cold butter, continuing to toss until noodles are well-coated—the sauce should thicken slightly. Season to taste with salt and pepper. Top with Parmesan and high-quality extra-virgin olive oil and serve immediately.

Chicken Liver Dumplings

Lee Anne Wong calls these offal-based bites the "MVP in my dumpling arsenal." She credits the chicken livers, an often underrated organ meat, as the key to keeping these dumplings moist and juicy, no matter how you cook them—boiled, steamed, panfried, or deep-fried—these doughy morsels come out deliciously. Wong says they're a crowd-pleaser at parties, but try using this recipe in response to your next takeout craving.

YIELD: 30 DUMPLINGS

SOY-GINGER DIPPING SAUCE:
½ cup water
¼ cup soy sauce
¼ cup rice, black, or Chinese red vinegar

2 tablespoons ginger, peeled and finely julienned
1 tablespoon granulated sugar
3 scallions, both white and green parts, chopped, for garnish

DUMPLINGS:
3 ounces dark meat chicken, ground
⅓ cup garlic chives or Chinese chives, chopped ⅛-inch thick
1 tablespoon Shaoxing rice wine
1 tablespoon low-sodium soy sauce
1 teaspoon ginger, peeled and minced
½ teaspoon sugar
¼ teaspoon kosher salt
Pinch ground white pepper
3 ounces chicken livers, cleaned and trimmed
1 recipe dumpling dough or 60 round dumpling skins

Make the soy-ginger dipping sauce: in a small bowl, mix together all the ingredients until the sugar dissolves. Refrigerate and allow the ginger to macerate for at least 1 hour.

Make the filling: in a large mixing bowl, combine the ground chicken, garlic chives, Shaoxing, soy sauce, ginger, sugar, salt, and white pepper. Pulse the chicken livers in a food processor until chopped small, or chop by hand. Combine the livers with the rest of the ingredients until the filling is well combined.

Place 1 tablespoon of filling on each dumpling wrapper. Brush the edge of the dough with water and then immediately fold the circle in half and pinch all the way around to seal the dumpling. Alternatively, pinch opposite points from each quarter of the circle together at the top of the dumpling to form a four-pointed dumpling.

Choose your cooking method.

Boiled: bring a large pot of salted water to a boil over high heat. Add the dumplings in small batches, so as not to crowd the pot. Return to a boil and add ½ cup of cold water. Bring the water to a boil again and add another ½ cup of cold water. When the water boils for the third time and the dumplings float, remove the dumplings from the water and serve (the dumplings should take about 6 minutes to cook).

Steamed: steam the dumplings on a piece of greased parchment paper set over a boiling water bath until the filling and dumpling skins are cooked through, about 6 to 8 minutes.

Panfried: in a liquid measuring cup, mix 2 cups of water and 2 tablespoons of flour until the flour has dissolved into the water and the mixture is cloudy. Heat a small nonstick pan over medium-high heat. Add 1 tablespoon vegetable oil to the pan and place the dumplings in the pan, lined up next to each other. Cook until the bottoms of the dumplings turn golden brown, about 1 to 2 minutes. Add ½ cup of the flour-water mix to the pan; it will react with the hot pan and steam and splatter a bit, so be ready with a tight-fitting lid. As soon as you add the flour-water mixture, cover the pan with the lid. Cook the dumplings, covered, until almost all of the water has evaporated and a thin golden crust begins to form in the bottom of the pan, about 3 minutes. Remove the lid and cook until all the water has evaporated, about 3 more minutes. Carefully remove the dumplings from the pan and serve immediately. Wash the pan and repeat with remaining dumplings and flour-water mixture. Be sure to keep stirring the flour and water slurry periodically since the flour will sink.

Deep-fried: preheat a large pot of canola or vegetable oil to 350°F. Carefully drop the dumplings one by one into the hot oil, frying in small batches and making sure not to overcrowd the pot. Cook the dumplings for 3 minutes, until the exterior is golden brown. Drain on a paper towel-lined plate. Repeat with remaining dumplings until all are cooked, making sure the oil temperature returns to 350°F before frying the next batch.

Scatter the cooked dumplings with the chopped scallions and serve immediately with the soy-ginger dipping sauce on the side.

BASIC DUMPLING DOUGH/FRESH WHEAT FLOUR DOUGH:

This dough is great for all types of cooking: boiling, steaming, panfrying, deep-frying. The hot water/liquid provides elasticity to the dough and shape retention to the wrapper. The dough can be rolled to desired thickness, depending on how you are using it. The amount of liquid you add will vary depending on humidity, altitude, and other environmental factors, but chef Wong likes to go by feel. While the dough can easily be made in a food processor, she prefers making it by hand because over time, one can know when the dough is right when it is soft and pliable to the touch. Both ways work. All-purpose flour works best as it has a medium level of gluten, which will provide body and elasticity without being too tough or chewy.

YIELD:

Roughly 1 pound of dough, enough for
      24 large dumplings or 32 medium
      dumplings
¾ cup to 1 cup water
2 cups (300g) all-purpose flour
1 teaspoon sesame oil or vegetable oil
Pinch of kosher salt

Bring the water to a boil. Remove from the heat and allow the water to sit for 1 minute. Place the flour in a large bowl and make a well in the center. Pour ¾ cup hot water and the sesame oil into the well and stir with a wooden spoon until well incorporated with the flour. Add more water by the teaspoon (as necessary) to make the dough come together. There will be small lumpy pieces but the dough should not be sticky. Gently bring the warm dough together in the bowl by kneading the pieces until you get a large mass. (Alternately: if using a food processor, place the flour in the bowl and turn the machine on. Add the hot water and oil to the flour in a thin, steady stream until everything is incorporated. Stop the food processor immediately and check that the dough has come together and is soft and pliable. If it is too dry, add water by the teaspoonful, pulsing the food processor until the dough comes together.)

Turn the dough out onto a work surface and knead into a uniform, soft, smooth mass; about 30 seconds to a minute for machine-made dough and 2 to 3 minutes for handmade dough. The dough will be smooth, elastic, and feel very dense but pliable. It should not be sticky at all and should bounce back slowly when you press your finger into it, leaving a shallow impression of your finger.

Wrap the dough in plastic wrap or place in a resealable plastic bag. Allow the dough to rest for at least 15 minutes and up to 3 hours at room temperature. At this point you can make your wrappers or refrigerate your dough for up to 2 days. Before using, allow your dough to warm to room temperature, as it will be easier to manipulate.

To make wrappers, roll the dough until it is ⅛-inch thick. Cut into rounds using a 4-inch round cutter. Use immediately to assemble dumplings.

Smoked Fish Mousse

Transform your weekend bagel platter leftovers into a stunning appetizer with this recipe from Cathal Armstrong. Smoked whitefish trimmings take a spin in a blender with rich cream cheese, cream, and butter, to make a decadent mousse that lets the fish flavor shine through. Armstrong serves it alongside crispy ciabatta and a salad with beets, radishes, and avocado.

YIELD: 4 CUPS

½ pound smoked white fish trim, cleaned of skin and veins
¾ cup cream cheese
¼ cup cream
1 cup (2 sticks) butter, cut into 1-inch cubes
Salt to taste

Put the fish, cream cheese, and cream in a blender and puree until it is smooth and no longer grainy. Add the butter gradually until all incorporated and the mousse is shiny and has a velvety consistency. Season with salt.

Refrigerate for at least 1 hour. Let stand at room temperature for at least 15 minutes to soften before serving.

Schmaltz Mashed Potatoes

Food waste is top of mind at Josh Kulp's Honey Butter Fried Chicken, where composting, recycling, and tracking waste are daily activities. That mentality extends to the menu, where necessity is the mother of delicious invention. Case in point: these ultra-creamy mashed potatoes. Kulp takes the restaurant's excess chicken bones and roasts them, collecting the fat, or "schmaltz" to whip into the potatoes, then using the bones for a stock that forms the base of the gravy as a final coup de grâce.

YIELD: 4 TO 6 SERVINGS

SCHMALTZ:
3 cups roughly chopped chicken
    skin and fat
½ cup water

CHICKEN FAT GRAVY:
⅓ cup schmaltz (rendered chicken fat)
⅓ cup plus 1 tablespoon all-purpose
    flour
1 quart chicken stock (preferably made
    with leftover chicken bones)
1 teaspoon minced rosemary leaves
Salt and pepper to taste

MASHED POTATOES:
3 pounds red potatoes
¾ cup heavy cream
¼ cup schmaltz
2 tablespoons unsalted butter
Salt and pepper to taste
Chicken fat gravy
Lemon zest

Make the schmaltz: combine the chicken skin and fat with water in a small pot and set over medium-low heat. Stir occasionally and cook at a bare simmer for 1 hour. Increase the temperature to medium and continue to cook the mixture until the pieces of skin and fat have browned slightly, approximately 15 minutes. Remove from the heat and strain the mixture over a bowl. The strained fat in the bowl is about 2/3 of a cup of ready-to-use schmaltz. The crispy bits in the strainer are called gribenes (or chicken cracklings) and are delicious in their own right as a snack or sprinkled over mashed potatoes or in chicken salad.

Make the gravy: in a medium pot over medium heat, add the schmaltz. Add the flour, mix well, and cook for approximately 3 to 5 minutes, stirring constantly with a wooden spoon to prevent scorching. Working in stages, add the chicken stock while whisking to combine. After whisking the mixture until smooth, continue to add more stock. Bring the gravy to a simmer and continue stirring until the gravy has thickened slightly, about 10 minutes. Add the rosemary and salt and pepper to taste.

Make the potatoes: in a pot filled with cold water, add the potatoes and a handful of salt and bring to a boil. Boil the potatoes and cook until fork tender, about 30 minutes. While the potatoes boil, in a separate pot, combine the heavy cream, schmaltz, and butter over low heat and keep warm.

When the potatoes are fork tender, drain them and transfer to a large bowl. Using a potato masher or a sturdy large fork, smash the potatoes. If smoother potatoes are desired, pass the potatoes through a potato ricer or food mill.

Add the warm cream, schmaltz, and butter mixture to the potatoes and use a spatula to combine. Season with salt and pepper to taste. Serve immediately topped with the chicken fat gravy and a fresh grating of lemon zest.

3.

Tops & Bottoms, Pits & Peels

Tips

1   Make veggie stock with wilting produce or the trimmings from vegetable prep. Keep everything in a resealable plastic bag or container in the freezer until you have enough to make stock.

2   Store Parmesan rinds in a resealable plastic bag in the freezer and toss into soups and broths to make them more flavorful and delicious.

3   Take the parts of your ingredients that usually get tossed in the garbage or compost, such as broccoli stems and turnip tops, and sauté them in a pan with olive oil and garlic.

4   Buy a juicer and turn your vegetable scraps into juice, either for drinking or as a base for sauces.

5   Instead of throwing away leek and scallion ends, plant them in your windowsill in a shallow cup of water. The stalks will regrow and you can use them again within a week or two, depending on conditions. Place the ends root-side-down in a cup and just barely submerge in clean water. Place the cup in the window and monitor every few days to replace the water as needed. (Clean water is essential.)

Broccoli Stem

Vinaigrette

When it comes to broccoli, it can be hard to see the forest for the trees. While the florets get most of the attention, the stems can also be a versatile tool to have in your culinary arsenal. Use them as the base for this spicy, earthy vinaigrette, which can be used on roasted potatoes or broccoli florets, grilled fish or chicken, or as part of a relish.

YIELD: 1 ½ CUPS

1 cup broccoli stems (about 1-inch-thick stem of broccoli), finely minced
1 hot pepper (jalapeño or serrano; pickled peppers are good, too!), minced
2 cloves garlic, minced (sub green garlic or garlic scapes in the spring)
Juice and zest of 2 lemons
¼ cup olive oil
1½ tablespoons grain mustard
1 tablespoon anchovy paste (optional)
Salt and pepper to taste

In a large bowl, mix the broccoli stems, pepper, and garlic together. (Alternatively, roughly chop the broccoli stems, pepper, and garlic and add to a food processor. Pulse a few times until the vegetables are minced, making sure to not overprocess them.) Add in the remaining ingredients and season to taste with salt and pepper.

Strawberry, Watermelon, Kale Salad

Sometimes all you need to turn scraps into a slamdunk is a flavor-packed sauce. In this recipe, Kenny Gilbert gives overripe fruit and wilted kale new life with a Cajun-inflected dressing that balances heat with the cooling power of fresh mint. Best of all, this versatile dressing works with whatever seasonal fruit and greens you've got sitting in your crisper, which means this salad can be your go-to recipe any time you need to clean out the refrigerator.

YIELD: 2 SERVINGS AS A SIDE OR 1 AS AN ENTRÉE SALAD

DRESSING:
3 tablespoons fresh lemon juice
2 tablespoons extra-virgin olive oil
¼ teaspoon Cajun spice
   (such as Ragin' Cajun)
2 tablespoons mint leaves, chopped

SALAD:
1 cup cubed watermelon
1 cup strawberries, quartered
¾ cup Tuscan baby kale, julienned
¼ cup thinly sliced red onions
2 tablespoons Cotija cheese, crumbled

Make the dressing: place lemon juice, oil, Cajun spice, and mint in a large bowl and mix well. Set aside.

Prepare the salad: add watermelon, strawberries, kale, and red onion to a bowl and mix together gently. Toss with the dressing, place salad into 2 bowls, and top with Cotija cheese.

Kale Stem

Crackers

Don't toss your kale stems after using the leaves! These crackers feature thin slices of tough kale stems throughout the dough. With no leavening involved, this recipe can easily be batched up or down, making it perfect for solo snacking or a unique addition to your next cheese platter. If you don't have a pasta maker, you can also roll the dough out very thin with a rolling pin. If you want more uniform crackers, you can use a sharp knife or pizza cutter to slice the dough into squares before baking.

YIELD: APPROXIMATELY 36 CRACKERS (DEPENDING ON SIZE)

2 cups kale stems (from 1 bunch kale), thinly sliced
1 tablespoon butter
1 teaspoon fine sea salt, divided
2 cups unbleached all-purpose flour
½ cup buttermilk
3 tablespoons olive oil, divided
2 teaspoons flaky sea salt

Cook the kale stems: set a wide skillet over medium heat and melt the butter. Add the kale stems and ½ teaspoon fine sea salt and cook until the stems are tender and bright green, about 2 minutes. Transfer the cooked, still warm stems to a food processor and pulse until a rough, chunky paste is formed. Remove the kale mixture from the food processor and spread out on a baking sheet to cool, about 20 minutes.

Prepare the dough: place the flour and remaining ½ teaspoon salt in a stand mixer fitted with a dough hook attachment. Add the kale stem mixture and turn the mixer on its lowest setting until the flour and kale are incorporated. With the motor running, slowly pour in half of the buttermilk. Let the dough come together and continue to add buttermilk slowly until a ball forms. (You may not need all of the buttermilk, depending on how much moisture is in the kale mixture.) Once a ball forms, turn the mixer off and remove the dough from the bowl. Knead the dough by hand for 1 minute, then cut into 2 pieces and wrap each piece individually with plastic wrap. Refrigerate the portioned dough and let rest overnight.

Make the crackers: preheat the oven to 350°F. Place a piece of parchment paper on a baking sheet and brush liberally with 1½ tablespoons olive oil. Run a portion of the dough through a pasta roller set to a ½-inch-thick setting. Run it again set to a ¼-inch-thick setting. Cut the dough into a length that will fit the baking sheet. Brush with the remaining olive oil and sprinkle lightly with flaky sea salt. Bake for 10 to 12 minutes, or until the crackers are light golden brown. Remove from the oven and let cool. Break into rough-edged crackers. Serve warm or at room temperature. Once cooled, you can store in an airtight container for several days.

Charred Broccoli Stems

with
Anchovy Vinaigrette

Oft-discarded broccoli stems are the star of this delicious side dish, which pairs them with chile, almonds, preserved lemon, and an umami-forward vinaigrette. Maria Hines tames the stems' tough texture with a quick sear in canola oil, which she recommends for its high smoke point and neutral flavor.

YIELD: 6 SERVINGS

CHARRED BROCCOLI:
¼ cup raw, halved almonds
6 broccoli stems
2 tablespoons canola oil
½ teaspoon garlic, minced
Pinch of chile flakes
Juice from ½ lemon
Salt to taste
1 tablespoon preserved lemon, thinly sliced (see recipe on page 190)

ANCHOVY VINAIGRETTE:
3 anchovy fillets packed in olive oil, drained
1 tablespoon white wine vinegar
⅛ large shallot, peeled and cut into chunks
¼ teaspoon ice water
3 tablespoons canola oil
Salt and pepper to taste

Make the charred broccoli: preheat the oven to 350°F. Spread the almonds out on a small baking sheet and toast in the oven until they're lightly golden brown, 7 to 10 minutes.

Peel the broccoli stems to remove the hard outer layer. Slice the stalks into thin slices to sear.

Add the oil to a heavy-bottomed frying pan set over medium-high heat. When the pan is hot, almost at its smoking point, add the stems and sear for about 20 seconds. (Depending on the size of your pan, you might need to work in batches—you won't want to add more than a single layer so that each piece can caramelize evenly.) Season the broccoli with salt and let it sit for about a minute. Flip the stems over and season with another sprinkle of salt.

Once both sides are seared, about 2 minutes total, add the garlic and chile flakes, and stir. Add the lemon juice and ¼ cup water to the pan and season with a pinch of salt. Once the liquid evaporates, about 5 minutes, the broccoli should be tender.

Make the anchovy vinaigrette: add the anchovy fillets, vinegar, shallots, and water to a blender. While the machine is on, slowly pour in the canola oil until the vinaigrette has thickened and emulsified. Season to taste with salt and pepper.

Transfer the charred broccoli to a serving platter, drizzle with the anchovy vinaigrette, and garnish with the preserved lemon and toasted almonds.

Green-Top

Harissa

A fiery North African condiment gets a waste-reducing revamp in this rendition from Levon Wallace. He supplements the traditional dried spice blend with root vegetable tops and herb stems, turning the typically ruby-hued spread a vibrant green. Use it to marinate chicken, spread on turkey burgers or grilled fish, or mix with Greek yogurt for an unexpected, flavorful dipping sauce.

YIELD: 2 CUPS

2 tablespoons cumin seeds
1 tablespoon coriander seeds
3 cups packed radish tops
    (or turnip tops, beet tops, etc.)
½ cup cilantro stems, finely chopped
½ cup parsley stems, finely chopped
½ cup olive oil
¼ cup lemon juice
6 to 8 scallion bottoms (the white
    and light green portion), sliced
2 jalapeño peppers, seeded and sliced
1 clove garlic, smashed
1 teaspoon kosher salt

Toast the cumin and coriander seeds in a small, dry skillet over medium-low heat, tossing constantly until very fragrant, about 3 minutes.

Place all ingredients in a food processor or blender, and process until smooth. Transfer the harissa to a nonreactive container with plastic wrap or parchment paper on the surface (this will keep the harissa from browning).

Note: The harissa can be made ahead and refrigerated for up to 4 days.

Rainbow Chard Noodles

Rainbow chard is a beautiful leafy green with tons of flavor. At Nick's, Derek Wagner's restaurant in Providence, Rhode Island, the chef uses the colorful, flavorful but rarely used chard stems in a number of ways, including shaving, dicing, slicing, and pickling. In this recipe, Wagner cuts the stems into strips and cooks them as you would pasta. This method also works well with beet stems.

YIELD: 2 CUPS COOKED CHARD NOODLES

1 bunch rainbow chard stems
Kosher salt
Ice water for shocking

Put a pot of water on the stove to boil and salt generously.

Trim the chard stems into strips that are approximately the same length and width. Add the stems to the boiling water and cook for about 10 minutes, until tender. Remove from heat, strain, and shock in an ice water bath to stop the cooking. Serve in any of the following preparations:

— Toss the cooked stems with butter and herbs; or add crumbled goat, feta, or blue cheese and garnish with toasted bread crumbs, toasted walnuts, or toasted whole grains such as rye seed, wheat berries, quinoa, or spelt.

— Toss cooked stems with a sauce of your choice, as you would pasta. Add them to spaghetti to lighten it up, or replace pasta with the chard noodles for a gluten-free meal.
— Stir-fry the chard with ginger, garlic, scallions, basil, cilantro, and chiles (pictured). Serve with or in place of noodles in Japanese, Korean, Thai, or Chinese stir-fries or soups.
— Layer the cooked chard stems into a frittata with sweet corn, greens, and cheese.

Creamy

Radish Leaf

Soup

This silky, elegant soup from JBF Award winner Rick Bayless lets radish leaves shine as the star ingredient. The leaves have a slightly peppery flavor, which Bayless complements with potatoes, butter, and rich crème fraîche, for a balanced, sophisticated appetizer. This recipe also works with turnip greens or other vegetables tops.

**YIELD: ABOUT 6 CUPS
(OR 6 TO 8 SERVINGS)**

3 tablespoons butter
2 bunches radishes with fresh-
    looking leaves
1⅓ pounds Yukon gold potatoes
    (4 to 5 medium), peeled and
    cut into about 1-inch pieces
5 cups chicken broth, plus a little
    more if needed
½ teaspoon ground white pepper

Salt to taste
⅓ cup crème fraîche, sour cream,
    or yogurt, plus more for serving
Lemon juice for serving

Prep the radishes: cut the leaves off the radishes right where stem joins the radish. Refrigerate the radishes for another use. Sort through the leaves and discard any wilted or yellow ones. Wash and dry the leaves in a salad spinner or on towels. You need about 6 cups lightly packed.

Wilt the radish leaves: set a medium-large (5- to 6-quart) saucepan or small soup pot over medium heat. Add the butter and let melt. Add the radish leaves and cover with a lid. Cook the leaves, stirring every once in a while, until completely wilted, about 15 minutes.

Add the chopped potatoes and chicken broth to the pot. Cover the pot,

keeping the lid slightly askew to allow steam to escape. Simmer until the potatoes are fall-apart tender, about 30 minutes.

Turn off the heat and use an immersion blender to blend soup until smooth. (If you don't have an immersion blender, use a regular blender. Fill the blender jar only half full, remove the center from blender top, secure top, cover with kitchen towel, and blend until smooth. When the first batch of the soup is blended, pour it back into the pot and continue with another batch.) Stir in the pepper, about 1 teaspoon salt (depending on saltiness of the broth), and the crème fraîche, sour cream, or yogurt. Add more broth if you think soup is too thick. Taste and add more pepper and salt if you think necessary. Ladle into soup bowls, top with a dollop of crème fraîche and a squeeze of lemon juice, and serve.

Zero-Waste Broth

Faced with the mountain of peels, skins, and trimmings created by East Coast chain Dig Inn's kitchens each day, culinary director Matthew Weingarten created this versatile broth, which turns a prodigious pile of produce scraps into a stock that can be poured over a bowl of grains and vegetables, or savored on its own.

YIELD: 7 CUPS

1 pound Spanish onions
    (about 1 large onion), chopped
½ pound carrots (about 4 small
    to medium carrots), chopped
2 tablespoons olive oil

1 pound (about 2 ½ cups) mixed
    root vegetable peels and scraps
    (except for sweet potatoes,
    which can make the broth too
    sweet), washed
¼ pound stems and brown gills
    from mushrooms
Cores (and skin) from 2 apples
2 cloves skin-on garlic, smashed
Tops and tails from 1 celery head
Stems from one bunch kale
1 (6-inch) piece of kombu
1 ounce dried shiitake mushrooms
6 whole black peppercorns
1 star anise pod
Sea salt to taste

Preheat the oven to 500°F. Toss the chopped onions and carrots in the olive oil and place on a baking sheet in a single layer. Place in the hot oven to roast until charred and caramelized, about 15 minutes.

Add the caramelized onions to a large pot with the remaining ingredients. Cover with 2 quarts water and bring to a gentle boil. Reduce heat to simmer and slowly cook for another 30 minutes. Add salt to taste. Strain the broth thoroughly using a fine mesh sieve. Serve immediately or cool down and store in the freezer in quart-size containers until ready to use.

Veggie Burgers

JBF Award winner Jonathon Sawyer calls this veggie burger his "meatless wonder," a tornado of tremendous flavor that sucks up juicing pulp, over- or underripe vegetables, and leftover rice. This genius patty even yields a pink center (courtesy of beets) that can only be called medium-rare.

YIELD: 10 TO 12 6-OUNCE PATTIES

4 cups cooked long-grain brown rice (ideally from leftovers!)
3½ cups pulp from juicing approximately 10–12 beets (or:
2 turnips, peeled and roughly chopped
1 large red beet, peeled and roughly chopped
1 bulb fennel, roughly chopped
1 small yellow onion, roughly chopped)
2 cloves garlic
Salt and pepper to taste
4 cups cooked white beans
½ cup rice flour, coconut flour, or all-purpose flour
¼ cup grapeseed or other high-heat oil
¾ cup mayonnaise
2 tablespoons capers

Grilled brioche buns, lettuce, sliced tomatoes, sliced red onions, thinly sliced cucumbers, and mayonnaise to serve

Preheat your oven to 350°F.

Make the burgers: in a large pot, bring 3 quarts of water to a boil. Add cooked rice and cook for 10 minutes, or until the grains have puffed up and broken up a bit. (This gives a ground beef–like texture to the patty.) Drain the rice and let cool on a sheet tray.

If using the pulp from your juicer, measure out approximately 3½ cups. Use a food processor to blitz the onion and garlic and mix well with the pulp. If not using pulp, combine the garlic, turnips, beet, fennel, and onion in a food processor and pulse until the vegetables are minced. You should have approximately 4 cups total. Transfer the minced vegetables to a baking sheet and season with salt and pepper to taste. Roast until tender, about 20 minutes. Allow the vegetables to cool.

Puree the beans in a food processor until smooth. You may need to add a drizzle of olive oil to get them going. Gently mix the rice, roasted vegetables, and bean puree in a large bowl by hand. Add the rice flour to the mixture and incorporate. Portion the mixture into 6-ounce patties.

Cook the patties: heat a cast-iron skillet or grill pan over medium heat. Brush the pan with oil and sear the patties for 2 minutes until golden brown (work in batches if needed). Flip the patties and sear on the other side for another 2 minutes. In a small bowl, combine mayonnaise with capers. Spread the mayonnaise mixture on grilled brioche buns, place one patty in each of the buns, and serve with lettuce, tomato, red onion, thinly sliced cucumbers, or your favorite burger toppings.

Vegetable Paella

Chef Katie Button tracks the seasons through this vegetable paella recipe, which shifts with the harvest in summer, fall, winter, and spring. This flexible main dish makes use of whatever's hiding in your crisper drawer, letting the vegetables ground the dish, and using scraps to build a stock for the rice.

YIELD: 2 ENTRÉE SERVINGS

VEGETABLE SCRAP STOCK:
3 cups mushroom stems
3 cups onion scraps (not the paper)
1½ cups carrot scraps
6 cloves garlic
1½ cups vegetable scraps
    (celery ends, bell pepper tops)
¼ cup plus 1 tablespoon oil, divided
1 tablespoon tomato paste
½ cup white wine
2 quarts of water
8 parsley stems

AÏOLI:
1 large egg
1 clove garlic, peeled and smashed
1¼ teaspoons lemon juice
¼ teaspoon kosher salt
1 cup blended oil or olive oil

PAELLA:
3 tablespoons olive oil
1 artichoke, cleaned, choke removed,
    stem intact, and cut into quarters
    (see note)
¼ red bell pepper, sliced thinly
¼ green bell pepper, sliced thinly
Handful of mushrooms (any variety),
    cut into bite-size pieces
1 tablespoon onion, grated

2 cloves garlic, minced
¼ cup grated fresh tomato
2 pinches pimentón
4 cups vegetable scrap stock (If using
    Arborio, Calasparra, or another
    short grain rice instead, the
    amount of stock needed can
    be reduced to 3 cups)
1 cup paella rice, preferably Bomba
Salt and pepper to taste

EQUIPMENT:
12-inch paella pan (or a 10- to 12-inch
    sauté pan)

Make stock: preheat oven to 450°F. Toss mushroom, onion, carrot, garlic, and vegetable scraps in ¼ cup oil and spread on a baking sheet. Roast, stirring every 5 minutes, until they have taken on color, about 30 minutes.

In a saucepot, heat 1 tablespoon oil over medium heat. Add the tomato paste and stir continuously until caramelized, about 2 minutes. Add the roasted vegetable scraps and the white wine. Cook until the wine has reduced by half, about 1 minute. Add the water and parsley stems. Bring the stock to a boil and then reduce the heat to a simmer. Simmer for 1 hour, then strain through a fine mesh sieve.

Make the aïoli: combine the egg, garlic, lemon juice, and salt in a food processor. Turn the machine on and pour a little of the oil through the feed tube. Slowly add the remaining oil and process until it's all emulsified into the mixture. (Alternately, to make the aïoli by hand, push the garlic through a garlic press, then whisk with the egg, lemon juice, and salt. Whisk in the oil,

a drop at a time, to ensure an emulsification that won't break.) The aïoli can be refrigerated in an airtight container for up to 1 week.

Make the paella: heat the paella pan over medium-high heat with a little bit of oil. Sauté the artichokes, peppers, and mushrooms so that they get a little color on them, about 5 minutes. Remove vegetables from pan. Set aside. Add more oil and cook onion and garlic until golden brown, about 2 minutes. Add grated tomato and cook until tomato has caramelized and liquid has evaporated, about 3 minutes. Add the pimentón and vegetable stock. Bring to a boil, add rice, and stir. Bring liquid to a boil again and reduce heat to a simmer. Taste and season with salt. Add artichokes and reduce, about 10 minutes. Place remaining vegetables on top of the rice and continue to cook paella until the liquid has cooked out of the pan and it begins to stick to the bottom of the pan, about 15 minutes. Raise heat to high for the last 5 minutes to create the crust. Remove the pan from the heat and let stand 10 minutes before serving. Serve with aïoli.

Note: to clean and trim artichokes, using a serrated knife, cut off the top half of the artichoke and half of the stem. Carefully pull off the outer leaves, making your way into the center of the artichoke. Using a paring knife, clean the remaining tough remnants of leaves until you have a pale green heart. Halve, remove hairy center with a knife, and submerge in lemon water until ready to cook.

Parmesan Broth

with

Greens, Beans, and Pasta

You've sliced, shaved, and grated; and now you're left with the sorry, tough end of your Parmesan wedge. As tempting as it might be to chuck this seemingly useless chunk in the trash, the far better place to toss the tidbit is in the nearest pot and make a soup, as Sara Jenkins does in this brothy pasta dish. This recipe works for whatever greens are in season, proving that preserving your Parmesan rind is a smart move all year long. Store any Parmesan rinds in the freezer until you're ready to use them.

YIELD: 4 TO 6 SERVINGS

HOMEMADE CHICKEN STOCK:
5 medium carrots, roughly chopped
4 celery stalks, roughly chopped
1 large onion with peel, cut into 8 pieces
1 head garlic, cut in half crosswise
1 cup extra-virgin olive oil
3 to 4 leftover chicken carcasses
1 large bunch flat-leaf parsley
    (or stems from assorted soft herbs
    like parsley, dill, cilantro, etc.)
1 cup dry white wine

PARMESAN BROTH WITH GREENS, BEANS, AND PASTA:
10 cups homemade or store-bought
    chicken stock

8 ounces Parmesan cheese rinds
    (about 6 to 8 rinds)
½ cup dry soup pasta (such as ditalini,
    annelini, or orzo)
½ cup cooked white beans
4 cups loosely packed, tender cooking
    greens (such as spinach, chard,
    mustard greens, kale, or chicory),
    roughly cut into ¼- to
    ½-inch-wide ribbons
1 lemon

Make the homemade chicken stock: combine the carrots, celery, onion, garlic, and olive oil in a large stockpot or soup kettle and set over high heat. Cook, stirring, until the vegetables are browned, about 8 minutes. Add the chicken carcasses, parsley, wine, and just enough water to cover the chicken and vegetables (about 12 cups water).

Reduce the heat to medium-low. When the broth comes to a simmer, add 2 cups cold water (this technique will keep the stock cooking at a low simmer; the stock should never come to a rolling boil, as that simply redistributes impurities). Reduce the heat to low and allow the stock to gently simmer, checking every ½ hour or so to skim the surface of fat and add cold water as needed. The chicken and vegetables should always be barely covered with liquid. Cook until the stock is very rich, about 4 hours. You will have about 4½ quarts, so freeze leftovers in 1-cup and 1-pint containers to have a supply always at the ready.

Strain the stock, discarding the vegetables and bones. Refrigerate the stock for 2 to 3 days or freeze for up to 6 months until ready to use.

Make the Parmesan broth with beans, greens, and pasta: in a large pot, combine the broth and cheese rinds and bring to a light simmer over extremely low heat. Simmer for about 2 hours, or until the broth has reduced to about 8 cups. Strain the broth through a sieve and discard the rinds.

Bring the broth back to a simmer and add salt to taste. Add the pasta and cook until al dente, about 10 minutes. Add the cooked white beans and the greens. When the pasta is done, turn off the heat, taste, and adjust for seasoning. Grate the lemon zest directly over the pot and squeeze the lemon juice into the soup. Serve immediately.

Smothered Beet, Carrot, and Turnip Greens

Use whatever leafy green you have on hand—kohlrabi tops, collard greens, broccoli leaves, and more—to make this straightforward, weeknight-friendly side dish. Spoon over rice or potatoes for a warming, hearty addition to your table. The stems and other scraps from the chopped vegetables can be reserved in a bag in the freezer to make vegetable broth.

**YIELD: 6 TO 8 SERVINGS
(ABOUT 6 CUPS)**

6 cups greens, finely chopped tops (from 1 bunch beets, 1 bunch turnips, and 1 bunch carrots, leaves), stems removed and reserved for vegetable broth
¼ cup leftover fat (such as bacon or chicken fat)
⅓ cup all-purpose flour
1 cup yellow onion, thinly sliced (about ½ medium onion), ends and peels reserved for vegetable broth
1 tablespoon garlic, minced
2 cups vegetable broth
1 tablespoon Worcestershire sauce
2 teaspoons kosher salt
1 teaspoon crushed red pepper

Prep the greens: remove the larger woody stems from all the greens; wash the greens thoroughly and reserve stems for the vegetable broth. Drain but do not shake dry, as the extra moisture will help wilt the greens. Chop the greens into 1-inch strips. Chop the carrot tops more finely, into ½-inch pieces, being careful to remove the woody stems. Separate the stems and other scraps from the leaves, and reserve for vegetable broth, if desired.

Make the smothered greens: in a 4-quart stainless steel or enamel pot with tight-fitting lid, heat the fat over medium-heat until hot but not smoking (a grain of rice dropped in the oil should sizzle briskly). Add the flour and, using a wooden spoon, stir quickly and constantly to make a roux, continuing until the flour browns to the color of peanut butter, 6 to 8 minutes.

Add the onions and garlic and stir into the flour mixture to sweat, stirring constantly until the aroma of onion and garlic with the toasty roux fills the room. Turn off the heat for a moment and slowly add the vegetable broth, stirring constantly until incorporated and the mix starts to look like a brown gravy. Return the heat to medium and bring to a boil, then add as many greens as you can fit in the pot. Add the Worcestershire, salt, and red pepper.

Lower the heat to medium-low and cook, stirring every 3 to 4 minutes with a wooden spoon to reach the bottom of the pot and turn the cooked greens over the top and raw greens underneath, then punch the whole pot of greens down to make room for more. Add as many greens as will fit into the pot, and repeat until all greens are in the pot. Add additional stock, a couple of tablespoons at a time as needed, but be patient to give the greens time to wilt and fall back into the gravy.

Once the greens are all wilted and bathing in gravy, cover the pot and continue to cook until the greens are thoroughly cooked and tender, which will take as little as 15 minutes for young, tender greens or up to an hour for larger, sturdier greens. Taste for seasoning and add more salt and pepper if desired.

Core Values
Chutney

You'd never know it, but this herby, nutty, and bright chutney is powered by the oft-discarded leaves, stems, and cores of cruciferous veggies like cauliflower, broccoli, and cabbage. Whip up a batch and use it as a spread on seafood, tacos, or enchiladas, as a dipping sauce for crudité, or folded into grains for a fresh punch of flavor.

YIELD: APPROXIMATELY 4 CUPS

1 pound leaves, stems, and cores of broccoli, cabbage, or cauliflower (or a mix), washed
1 cup nuts (such as almonds, cashews, or peanuts), toasted
3 lemons, zested and juiced
3 limes, zested and juiced
4 cloves garlic, peeled
½ cup extra-virgin olive oil
¼ cup honey
¼ cup white or golden balsamic vinegar
2 tablespoons skin-on ginger, minced
2 tablespoons Dijon mustard
1 bunch basil leaves with tender stems, washed
1 bunch cilantro with stems, washed and roughly chopped
1 bunch flat-leaf parsley with stems, washed and roughly chopped
1 jalapeño (with seeds), chopped
Granulated sugar, as needed
Kosher salt and freshly ground black pepper to taste

Prepare the vegetables: gently boil the broccoli, cabbage, or cauliflower leaves, stems, and cores in a large pot of salted water. Cook until the vegetables are tender, about 18 minutes. Drain well and cool to at least room temperature.

Make the chutney: in a food processor, grind the nuts until they are a fine crumb. Add the citrus juices and zest, garlic, olive oil, honey, vinegar, ginger, and mustard. Process well. Add remaining ingredients, including the boiled vegetables. Puree well. Taste the chutney and adjust the salt and sugar levels, as desired.

Apple or Pear Scrap Jelly

This gorgeous jelly is sure to impress your family and friends without them ever knowing the secret ingredient is actually leftovers: the cores, peels, and bruised pieces of apples or pears. JBF Award winner Steven Satterfield serves this at his restaurant alongside chicken rillettes, but this preserve also pumps up a pedestrian PB&J.

YIELD: APPROXIMATELY 2 CUPS

4 cups apple or pear scraps
        (cores, peels, bruised fruit, etc.)
2 cups apple cider
2 cups water
1 cup apple cider vinegar
1 cup granulated sugar
¼ cup cranberries (fresh or frozen)
½ teaspoon fine sea salt

Combine apple (or pear) scraps, apple cider, water, vinegar, sugar, cranberries, and salt in a medium saucepot. Cook on medium until solids are soft and falling apart, about 30 minutes.

Transfer the mixture to a fine mesh sieve and strain over a large bowl to catch the liquid. Do not press down on the solids as they drain and allow to strain for 30 minutes.

Discard the solids, then return the remaining liquid back into the saucepot and cook over medium heat until reduced by three-quarters and large, slow bubbles form, about 20 minutes.

Remove from the heat and let cool. Once the jelly is cool, check the viscosity. If it's loose, return the mixture to the pan and cook over medium heat one more time until large bubbles form. (Be careful not to cook the jelly to the point of caramelizing. Watch out for nutty smells—it should smell like bright apples while cooking.) Store in the refrigerator for two weeks, or preserve using the method below.

While the jelly is cooking, sterilize jars in a water bath by submerging the jars in simmering water in a large pot lined with a jar rack. Keep in water for 5 minutes then carefully pull out with tongs and set upside down on a clean work space to dry.

Sweet Corn Stock

Save a little bit of summer by using the husks, silks, and cobs from ears of seasonal corn. To really capture the grain's essence, Jamie Simpson boils down the usually discarded parts of corn, creating a rich and subtly sweet stock with myriad uses, from purees and soups to margaritas and even as the base of a Sweet Corn Sorbet (page 126).

YIELD: 12 CUPS

6 ears of corn, cobs, husks, and silks (strip off corn and freeze for future use, or in Vanilla Creamed Corn recipe on page 125)
Water

Wash the corn husks well and discard the tough, outermost leaves.

In a stock pot large enough to hold the contents of your corn by-products, submerge the cobs, husks, and silks. Bring the water to a boil, partially cover with a lid, and then lower the heat to a low simmer. Cook for about an hour.

Strain the stock through a fine mesh sieve and chill in the refrigerator. Store for up to a week in the refrigerator; and several months in the freezer. Reserve the stock for purees, soups, poaching liquids, grits or polenta, risotto, granita, or even margaritas.

Vanilla Creamed Corn

Unlike typical creamed corn, which puts kernels on a pedestal, Simpson's recipe is an equal-opportunity employer of the grain's multiple flavor-yielding parts. He simmers the kernels with a cup of his scrap-centered stock (page 124), then tosses in all manner of cream, butter, and vanilla for a luscious, silky ode to the summer.

YIELD: 1 QUART

4 tablespoons butter, diced
2 ears fresh corn kernels (or a 10-ounce
    bag of frozen kernels)
1 cup corn stock (see page 126)
½ cup cream
2 tablespoons milk
1 tablespoon sugar
¼ of a vanilla bean, scraped
⅛ teaspoon nutmeg
Large pinch sea salt

In a medium sauté pan or small saucepan, simmer the corn, corn stock, and butter together until the corn is very tender, about 5 minutes. Transfer the mixture to a blender and process on high until smooth. Add the cream, milk, sugar, scraped vanilla, nutmeg, and salt to the blender and blend on high for an additional minute. Strain through a fine mesh sieve.

Serve as a side dish, or whip equal parts room-temperature butter into the creamed corn and chill for an amazing spreadable condiment for cornbread.

Sweet Corn Sorbet

Jamie Simpson's husk-and-cob corn stock (page 124) is good for a wide variety of dishes, from appetizer to dessert, and all that's in between. In this recipe, Simpson leans on his sweet tooth, using the stock to make a simple sorbet that lets the grain speak for itself.

YIELD: 1 QUART

4 cups corn stock (page 124)
1 cup sugar
1½ teaspoons potato starch (optional)
1 teaspoon salt

In a saucepan set over low heat, add the corn stock and sugar. Cook until the sugar is dissolved, about 3 minutes if the stock is hot, or 5 to 7 minutes if the stock is cold. Let cool.

In a bowl, whisk all ingredients together until smooth. Transfer all ingredients to a small or medium saucepot. Bring the mixture to a simmer and whisk well. Chill the mixture in the refrigerator or over an ice bath. Transfer to an ice cream maker and churn according to the manufacturer's directions. If you do not have an ice cream maker, freeze the base in a small pan and scrape with a fork to form a delicate granita.

Baked Potato Stock

with
Beurre Monté

Potato skins aren't just for game day anymore: Jamie Simpson has discovered a way to make the humble tuber's peels into a sensational stock that does wonders as the base of vegetable soups, chowders, and sauces. Add it to any dish that spotlights spuds, and you'll bump up the flavor tenfold—or mound with butter as Simpson does here for an over-the-top beurre monté to use as a sauce for vegetables or meat. Note: the stock recipe here yields more than you will use for the beurre monté, but you can freeze extra stock for future use.

BAKED POTATO STOCK:
YIELD: 6 CUPS STOCK
2 cups packed peels (from about
   5 pounds of potatoes)
3 tablespoons vegetable oil
Salt to taste

BAKED POTATO STOCK WITH
BEURRE MONTÉ:
1 cup baked potato stock
½ pound butter, diced
1 teaspoon salt

To make the stock: preheat the oven to 375°F. In a large bowl, lightly dress your potato peels in the vegetable oil. Spread the peels on a baking sheet and bake them in the oven until crispy and golden brown, about 30 minutes.

In a small pot, add the baked peels and just enough cold water to cover them (about 6 cups). Bring the pot up to a simmer and turn off the heat. Allow the stock to sit for 30 minutes. Strain through a fine mesh sieve and season to taste with salt.

To make the beurre monté: In a small saucepan, reduce one cup of the stock down by two-thirds of its original volume. Whisk in the butter 1 piece at a time until fully incorporated and emulsified. Remove from the heat and add the salt. Serve warm as a butter sauce over vegetables, fish, or meat.

Fruit Skin–Crusted Mahi-Mahi

This quartet of waste-reducing recipes can be served together or on their own. The foundation is a scrap-driven sofrito, and the remaining recipes are built on Mario Pagan's unusual fruit skin dust, a powder made from herbs, spices, and dried peels. He recommends storing fruit peels in the freezer until you're ready to use them.

YIELD: 4 SERVINGS

FRUIT SKIN DUST:
½ cup assorted fruit peels
    (like papaya, passion fruit,
    mango, orange, lemon, or lime)
1 whole cinnamon stick
½ whole star anise pod
½ teaspoon sage leaves
½ teaspoon mint leaves
½ vanilla bean, scraped

SOFRITO SWEET POTATO HASH:
6 cloves garlic
5 habanero peppers
4 sprigs rosemary
1 bunch scallions
1 bunch parsley
1 green bell pepper, seeded
1 red bell pepper, seeded
1 yellow bell pepper, seeded
1 leek
1 red onion
2 tablespoons honey
2 tablespoons olive oil

Salt and pepper to taste
1 large sweet potato

CITRUS–BALSAMIC CREAM:
1 tablespoon butter
1 tablespoon shallots, minced
⅔ cup fresh orange juice
⅓ cup balsamic vinegar
¼ cup heavy cream
2 tablespoons fresh lime juice
1 tablespoon Fruit Skin Dust
Salt to taste

MAHI-MAHI:
4 (6-ounce) skinless mahi-mahi
    fillets (also known as dorado
    in the Caribbean)
4 tablespoons grapeseed oil
Salt and pepper to taste
1 tablespoon Fruit Skin Dust

Make fruit skin dust: spread ingredients on a baking sheet. Place the baking sheet in a dry, preferably warm, area of your kitchen and let dry for three days. Once dry, grind everything in a food processor until you are left with a coarse powder. Sift powder through a fine mesh sieve, discarding solids and reserving the fine dust.

Make hash: preheat oven to 350°F. Place all the ingredients, except the sweet potato, in a food processor and blend until there are no large pieces, about 1 minute. Keep frozen for up to 1 week or refrigerate for immediate use.

Cut the sweet potato into ¼-inch dice. Place on a greased or nonstick sheet pan. Bake in the oven for 15 to 20 minutes, or until fork tender. Immediately transfer the sweet potatoes to a bowl and add 5 tablespoons sofrito. Mash the sweet potatoes and sofrito with a fork. Add salt and pepper to taste.

Make citrus–balsamic cream: in a small pot set over medium-high heat, add the butter and sauté the shallots until translucent, about 2 minutes. Add the liquids and cook until the sauce has reduced by ¾. Add the fruit skin dust and salt to taste. Set aside.

Cook mahi-mahi: in a medium sauté pan, heat oil over medium-high heat. Season fillets with salt and pepper to taste. Dust the topside of the fillets with about ¼ teaspoon of the Fruit Skin Dust on each fillet until they are completely covered. Carefully place the fillets dusted-side-down into the oiled pan and sear for 30 seconds. Flip the fillets and sear for another 30 seconds on the other side. Remove the fillets with a fish spatula and place on a sheet pan. Bake in the oven for 9 minutes, or until cooked through.

To serve, place hash in the shape of a hamburger patty, about 1-inch thick, on a plate. Place a fillet on top of the hash, then spoon the citrus–balsamic cream over the fillet.

Vegetable Salad

with
Pickle Vinaigrette

Consider this salad the supreme vegetable vacuum. It sucks up any old odds and ends in the fridge, from veggies that are best roasted (like potatoes or cauliflower) to those better off raw, to herbs and even fronds or tops. Abra Berens dresses this proliferation of produce in a dressing made of leftover pickle jar liquid. If you're really feeling ambitious, she recommends using up old cream by turning it into homemade sour cream or crème fraîche and mixing it in.

YIELD: 5 SERVINGS

5 fingerling potatoes, cut into wedges
¼ medium head cauliflower
2 teaspoons olive oil
Salt and pepper to taste
3 radishes
2 medium carrots, peeled
½ large head fennel
¼ medium head purple cabbage
½ bunch parsley, roughly chopped
½ bunch cilantro, roughly chopped
½ cup sour cream
¼ cup pickle liquid

Heat the oven to 400°F.

On a rimmed baking sheet, toss the potatoes and cauliflower with the olive oil and salt and pepper to taste. Roast until crispy outside and tender inside, 20 to 25 minutes.

Shave or cut the radishes, carrots, fennel, cabbage, and cauliflower thinly with a knife or mandolin.

In a large bowl whisk together the sour cream and pickle liquid. Add the raw and roasted vegetables and chopped herbs and toss together. Season with salt and pepper to taste. Taste and adjust the seasoning and acidity as desired.

Satsuma

Marmalade

This satsuma marmalade features only the skins of the fruit, which would normally end up in the garbage. Scented with cardamom, ginger, and vanilla, it's perfect for toast, scones, or thumbprint cookies. This recipe works for any fruit peels, such as grapefruit, oranges, limes, or lemons.

YIELD: 4 CUPS (ENOUGH FOR FOUR 8-OUNCE JELLY JARS)

6 cups water
½ cup Meyer lemon juice
    (about 4 lemons)
2 cups satsuma peels, julienned
    (about 2 pounds of satsumas)
1 pound of granulated sugar
½ teaspoon ground ginger
1 teaspoon ground cardamom
1 teaspoon vanilla extract
½ package pectin (optional)

In a large pot over medium heat, add water, lemon juice, and julienned satsuma peels. Bring to a boil, then reduce to a simmer. Simmer for 40 minutes, until peels are broken down and the mixture has thickened.

Bring the mixture back up to a boil, then add the sugar, ginger, cardamom, and vanilla extract. Stir very often, until mixture reaches about 223°F. (This will take another 30 minutes to 1 hour.) If your mixture can't quite reach 223°F, then use the half package of pectin to thicken.

While the marmalade is cooking, sterilize jars in a water bath by submerging the jars in simmering water in a large pot lined with a jar rack. Keep in water for 5 minutes then carefully pull out with tongs and set upside down on a clean work space to dry.

Once the marmalade is done, carefully scoop it into the sterilized jars, leaving a half inch of headspace. Seal with lids and return to the water bath. Simmer for another 10 minutes, then remove.

Place the jars upside down on a dishtowel on counter and allow to cool for several hours and up to overnight. If any lids don't "pop" and seal, place those jars in the refrigerator. The others can be stored at room temperature for up to six months.

Candied

Citrus Peels

This simple recipe to use up your citrus peels comes from the James Beard Foundation's own Mitchell Davis, who makes a batch a few times a year to use in his many home baking projects. They also make the perfect sweet-bitter snack, or a decadent dessert when dipped in dark chocolate. Save up citrus peels until you have enough to get about 2 to 3 cups of sliced peels so that you can make a batch that will last for months.

2 to 3 cups (¼-inch thick) sliced
    peels of citrus, such as grapefruit,
    orange, or lemon
2 cups sugar, plus extra for rolling
¼ cup corn syrup

Place the peels in a saucepan and cover with cold water. Bring to a boil, turn down the heat, and simmer for 7 to 8 minutes. Drain. Place the peels back in the pot and cover with cold water again. Bring to a boil, simmer for 7 to 8 minutes again, and drain. Repeat two more times for a total of 4 blanchings. If you are using grapefruits or other citrus with a thick layer of white pith, you can trim some of it off, if you'd like. Set the peels aside.

In the same saucepan, combine the sugar and corn syrup with 2 cups of water. The sugar and water mixture should cover the peels when you add them in the next step. Set over medium-high heat and bring to a boil, stirring to dissolve the sugar. Once sugar is dissolved, simmer for 5 minutes. Add peels and simmer gently for 30 minutes, until the peels are soft and almost translucent. Remove from the heat, cover, and let sit overnight.

The next day, gently heat again to melt the syrup. Lift the peels out of the pan, drain, and lay across a wire rack to dry for an hour or so. Spread extra sugar on a plate. Roll peels in sugar and return to the rack to dry out completely for a few more hours. Roll in sugar one more time, and store in an airtight container in the refrigerator. The peels will keep in the refrigerator for 6 months or more.

4.

Second-Day Solutions

Tips

Tuscan Bread and Tomato Soup

Pappa al pomodoro is one of those recipes that proves reducing food waste is not a modern concept. Traditionally, this Italian dish relies on pieces of stale bread to soak up broth and thicken the soup. In this iteration, Cathy Whims doubles down on thrift by adding leftover Parmesan rinds, kicking up the umami level and adding complexity to this comforting classic.

YIELD: 10 SERVINGS

2 tablespoons plus ¾ cup olive oil, divided
1 clove garlic, slivered
2 ¼ pounds ripe sweet tomatoes, peeled and seeded (or 1 pound plus 2 ounces canned plum tomatoes, squeezed and drained of most of their juices)
1 (2-inch) Parmesan rind
Sea salt and freshly ground black pepper to taste
1 loaf (12 ounces) stale Pugliese bread or other Italian bread
2 large sprigs basil
Extra-virgin olive oil for serving

Add the 2 tablespoons olive oil and garlic into a heavy saucepan and cook gently until fragrant, about 1 minute. Just before the garlic turns brown, add the tomatoes and the Parmesan rind. Simmer for 30 minutes, stirring occasionally, until the tomatoes become concentrated. Season with salt and pepper, then add ¾ cup water and bring to a boil.

Cut most of the crust off the bread and cut into large chunks, about 1–2 inch cubes. Put the bread into the tomato mixture and stir until the bread absorbs the liquid and becomes mushy, adding more boiling water if it is too thick. Remove from the heat and allow to cool slightly. If the basil leaves are large, tear them into smaller pieces. Stir the basil into the soup with ½ to ¾ cup extra-virgin olive oil. Let sit before serving to allow the bread to absorb the flavor of the basil and oil. Remove the Parmesan rind before serving.

Serve the soup either at the traditional room temperature or warm. Divide the soup into bowls and drizzle each serving with extra-virgin olive oil.

Beverly Brown's Potato Rolls

Howard Hanna says that many of his favorite dishes from around the world originated with grandmothers cooking frugally—and the chef makes good on his word with this dish, which hasn't left his restaurant's menu since its first appearance. These soft, fluffy, and subtly sweet rolls come courtesy of Hanna's sous chef Kara Anderson, who learned to make them at the knee of her grandmother, Ms. Beverly Brown herself. Instead of suffering through gummy rewarmed mashed potatoes, use your leftovers to make these irresistible rolls that have both the grandma and restaurant kitchen seal of approval.

YIELD: APPROXIMATELY 36 LARGE DINNER ROLLS

4 cups plus 1 tablespoon whole milk, divided
2 cups mashed potatoes
2 sticks butter, plus more for brushing on after baking
¾ cup sugar
2 teaspoons salt
3 teaspoons yeast
8 cups bread flour, divided
5 eggs, divided
Fleur de sel to taste

Combine the milk, mashed potatoes, butter, sugar, and salt in a saucepan. Heat on low heat until the butter has melted, whisking until the mixture is smooth, about 10 minutes—whisking constantly if butter is cold. Let cool about 1 hour, to room temperature.

In a small bowl, combine the yeast with 1 cup of the flour. Add the flour and yeast to the cooled milk mixture. Transfer the mixture to the bowl of a stand mixer fitted with a dough hook attachment. Add 2 more cups of flour and mix on medium speed. When the flour is incorporated, add eggs all at once, followed by the remaining flour. Mix until a dough ball has formed. Continue mixing until the dough is smooth, soft, and slightly sticky, about 10 minutes. Transfer the dough ball to a buttered bowl and cover with a slightly damp towel. Place the bowl in a warm part of your kitchen and let the dough rise until doubled in size, about 1½ hours.

To shape the rolls, first cover your hands in flour. Portion the dough into 2-ounce pieces, shape the rolls by rolling them in your hands, and transfer them to a parchment-lined baking sheet about 2 inches from one another. You should have 30 rolls, which will fit neatly on a large baking sheet arranged into 5 rows, or if you are using smaller baking sheets, you can separate onto two sheets. Allow the dough to rise again for about 30 minutes. They should increase in size until they are almost touching each other.

While the rolls are proofing, preheat the oven to 350°F. Whisk the last egg with 1 tablespoon milk and brush the rolls with the egg wash. Transfer to the oven and bake for 18 to 20 minutes. The rolls should have fused together to keep the sides lighter in color and super soft while the tops are beautifully golden. Brush generously with melted butter as soon as they come out of the oven. Sprinkle with fleur de sel and eat while they are hot.

Rotisserie

Chicken Cage Soup

Ashley Christensen promises it's not cheating to get a grocery store rotisserie chicken—in fact, she admits it's her "most relied-upon convenience" when she doesn't have the time or energy to make dinner. But even if you didn't roast the chicken yourself, you can still use the carcass (or the "cage") to make an exquisite soup. Christensen encourages you to go all-in on the scrap scouring, using the rest of your crisper drawer's odds and ends to flavor the broth, which is then poured around a fresh salad for a unique dish that's part soup and part salad.

Note: the broth here yields 2 quarts, though you only need 1 quart to make this recipe. We suggest freezing the leftovers to use anywhere you'd usually rely on chicken broth.

YIELD: 6 SERVINGS

BROTH:

2 ears corn, shucked, kernels reserved
    for salad recipe
1 large red onion, unpeeled
2 tablespoons canola or other neutral
    cooking oil
1 whole head garlic, cut across
    horizontally

1 (4-inch) knob ginger root, skin on
    and sliced into ¼-inch coins
1 celery root, cut into 8 pieces
    (or 2 stalks of celery, cut into
    1-inch pieces)
1 cup white wine
1 rotisserie chicken carcass (cage),
    majority of meat removed,
    and bones gently torn apart
Stems from 1 bunch of cilantro
1 large tomato, grated on a box grater
    (about 1½ cups grated tomato)
1 gallon water
Sea salt

SALAD:

1 cup cherry tomatoes, quartered
Sea salt to taste
Reserved corn kernels from 2 ears corn
    (1½ cups corn kernels)
1 jalapeño pepper,
    half finely minced and half
    thinly sliced for garnish
1 tablespoon red onion, finely minced
2 tablespoons loosely packed chopped
    cilantro, plus more for garnish
12 cracks of black pepper (¼ tsp.)
2 tablespoons extra-virgin olive oil
1 lime, cut in quarters, divided
Sea salt to taste
4 ounces queso fresco, crumbled
1 avocado, pitted, peeled, and
    thinly sliced

Make the broth: shuck the ears of corn. Save and reserve the silk threads (which will add sweetness to your broth) and discard the husks. Cut the kernels from the cobs and reserve for the salad. Slice the cobs into 1-inch coins. Remove the skin from the red onion and set aside. Slice the red onion into quarters through the root end. Reserve one-quarter of the onion for the salad.

In an 8-quart stock pot, warm the oil over medium-high heat until it shimmers. Add the garlic halves, 3 onion quarters, onion skin, ginger, celery or celery root, and corncob pieces, and sauté until caramelized, about 5 minutes. Add the white wine and deglaze the pan, scraping up any brown bits on the bottom. Let the wine reduce for 2 minutes and then add chicken cage pieces, cilantro stems, tomato, and reserved corn silk, and cover with the water. Increase the heat to high and bring to a boil. Reduce the heat to medium (you're looking for the liquid to vigorously simmer, but not a full rapid boil), and cook uncovered for 2½ hours. Season to taste with salt. Remove from the heat, and strain through a fine mesh sieve, discarding the solids.

The broth should yield about 2 quarts. Measure out 1 quart and set aside; reserve the rest for another use, letting cool completely before covering and freezing.

Make the salad: place the tomatoes in a medium bowl and season liberally with sea salt. (Note: season twice as heavily as you would season tomatoes for a sandwich. In addition to seasoning, this salt will coax the juice out of the tomatoes, a technique called "bleeding." This natural tomato juice will act in part like a vinaigrette for the salad.) Let the tomatoes sit with the salt for 5 minutes.

Add the reserved corn kernels, minced portion of the jalapeño, minced red onion, cilantro, cracked pepper, and olive oil. Gently toss everything together to mix and coat all of the ingredients. Squeeze the juice of 2 of the lime quarters over the bowl and add the crumbled queso fresco. Again, toss gently to incorporate the lime and the cheese (add the cheese last to keep it from breaking down). If necessary, season to taste with additional sea salt.

Assemble the dish: heat one quart of the broth with 1 teaspoon of sea salt.

Once the broth reaches a simmer, remove from heat and season with the juice of the remaining 2 lime quarters.

Divide the salad among 4 bowls. Top each with some of the sliced avocado, a few cilantro leaves, and (optionally) two slices of the remaining jalapeño half. Pour some of the hot broth to the side of the salad, allowing it to fill the bowl around the salad, and serve immediately.

Skillet Chilaquiles

Perfect for fostering creativity in the kitchen, this dish combines eternal favorites—chips and salsa—with vegetables and herbs straight from the garden. This recipe is not only quick and delicious; it's also a fantastic way to use up leftovers.

YIELD: 4 SERVINGS

2 cups chicken or vegetable broth
1 cup tomato salsa
½ cup half-and-half or heavy cream
6 to 8 cups corn tortilla chips
2 cups of your favorite vegetables (see ideas below)
1 cup cooked, leftover chicken, shredded (optional)
1 cup panela cheese (Cacique is a good brand), cut into ½-inch dice
1 ripe avocado, halved, pitted, peeled, and cut into ½-inch dice
1 to 2 jalapeño or serrano chiles,
stemmed, seeded if desired, and minced
½ small red onion, finely diced
½ bunch cilantro, chopped
1 lime, cut into wedges, for serving
¼ cup sour cream, for serving (optional)
4 fried eggs, for serving (optional)

VEGETABLE IDEAS:
— Sautéed zucchini and/or zucchini blossoms
— Roasted yams and caramelized onions
— Roasted poblano chiles and red, yellow, and green bell peppers
— Sautéed mixed mushrooms and fresh oregano or epazote
— Sautéed greens, such as collard greens, red chard, and/or green chard
— Grilled corn and black beans

In a wide skillet, bring the broth, salsa, and half-and-half or cream to a boil. Add the tortilla chips, vegetables, and chicken (if using), mixing gently to coat each chip while the sauce simmers.

In 1 to 2 minutes, when some of the chips have moistened and begun to break up but others are still holding their shape, add the panela cheese. Continue stirring gently for another minute to distribute the cheese evenly.

Add the avocado, chiles, onions, and cilantro and stir well to distribute. Cook for 1 minute, just to heat through, and then remove from the stovetop. Divide the chilaquiles among 4 warmed plates. Top with a squeeze of lime, a dollop of sour cream, and a fried egg. Serve immediately.

Gazpacho

In the heat of summer when running a blender is about all the cooking you can handle, this vibrant recipe from Border Grill chefs Mary Sue Milliken and Susan Feniger packs a one-two punch for warm-weather cooking woes. It makes use of an overabundance of summer produce at its peak and any stale bread that's lying around. Pro tip: be sure to use fresh garlic here, as the flavor of old garlic can dominate the soup.

YIELD: 1 QUART (4 SERVINGS)

1 ounce day-old bread
    (approximately one slice)
1 medium cucumber or 2 pickling
    or Kirby cucumbers, chopped
1 stalk celery, chopped
1 tomato, cored and quartered
½ small green bell pepper, cored
    and seeded
2 garlic cloves, peeled
1 jalapeño, seeds optional, roughly
    chopped
16 ounces fresh tomato puree
    (if it's not peak tomato season,
    substitute tomato juice)

Optional garnishes: chopped chives and chervil, diced tomatillo and tomato, and a drizzle of extra-virgin olive oil

In a bowl, soak the bread in water for 5 minutes to rehydrate. Squeeze out any excess water.

Put rehydrated bread in a blender and puree it with the cucumber, celery, tomato, green pepper, garlic, and jalapeño. Add the tomato puree (or juice) and process until smooth.

Serve in bowls with a garnish of chives, chervil, diced tomatillo and tomato, and a drizzle of olive oil.

Fish Croquettes

At his Chicago restaurant, Paul Fehribach buys whole fish and uses the heads and the backbones that don't make it to the diners' plates for stocks and sauces. But even after the stocks are made, some of the most flavorful meat of the fish remains. Fehribach and his team carefully pick the meat from the bones to make this recipe, but this dish easily translates to the home kitchen—just use a couple of fillets from last night's dinner and any leftover rice you have on hand.

**YIELD: 15 TO 20 FRITTERS
(ABOUT 6 TO 8 SERVINGS)**

1 cup short-grain rice such as carnaroli (or use about 2½ cups of leftover rice)

1 tablespoon vegetable oil, plus about 2 quarts for frying, divided

½ cup yellow onion, finely minced

½ teaspoon garlic, minced

¼ cup green onion tops, finely chopped

1 teaspoons kosher salt

½ teaspoon freshly ground black pepper

Pinch cayenne pepper

1 to 2 cups pulled fish meat, coarsely chopped

2 large eggs

⅓ cup cold water

½ pound homemade bread crumbs or panko

If you're making fresh rice, cook the rice in a 2-quart saucepan with a tight fitting lid, and have it hot and at the ready to make the croquette filling. If using leftover rice, steam to heat up for use in the next step.

In a 4-quart cast-iron Dutch oven, heat 1 tablespoon vegetable oil over high heat until smoking, then add the yellow onions and garlic. Working quickly and stirring constantly with a wooden spoon, sauté until the onions have sweat, but make sure not to brown the onions, about 2 minutes. Add the green onions, salt, black pepper, and cayenne pepper, then reduce the heat to low. Fluff the rice with the tines of a fork and add to the pot and stir in well.

Using the back of a wooden spoon, mash the rice a bit until everything begins sticking together. Add the pulled fish meat and turn the heat up to medium, stirring the mixture constantly to prevent burning while you work the fish in and bring everything up to 165°F on a food safety thermometer.

Transfer the mixture to a baking sheet with edges and spread out until it's about an inch thick. Let cool uncovered for 30 minutes. Cover tightly with plastic wrap and refrigerate for at least 1 hour or overnight before breading and frying.

Use a small ice cream scoop to shape the filling into balls, about 3 tablespoons each. Roll the mixture between the palms of your hands to smooth it out on all sides and place on a baking sheet with plenty of space between each ball. In a mixing bowl, beat the eggs until frothy with a wire whisk and then whisk in the water. Fill a large pie pan with bread crumbs and reserve any extra bread crumbs.

Roll each ball first in bread crumbs, then gently roll between your palms again to work crumbs into the filling. Roll the ball in the egg wash, wetting all sides, then roll in bread crumbs again. Roll a little more firmly after the second dip using your fingers and palms to finalize the fritter into a fat egg shape. Return the breaded croquettes to the baking sheet and repeat until all have been breaded. Refrigerate, covered loosely with plastic wrap, until ready to fry.

Use a home deep fryer or 4-quart cast-iron Dutch oven. If using a Dutch oven, fill with about 3 inches of vegetable oil. Heat oil to 325°F and watch the temperature closely to maintain as close to this frying temperature as possible. Gently drop the croquettes in a few at a time, making sure there is plenty of space between each ball—don't overcrowd or they may not brown evenly. Turn occasionally while cooking. Fry for 5 to 6 minutes, until the croquettes are a deep, rich, golden brown color. Remove with a slotted spoon and drain on paper towels. Keep in a low oven while you fry any remaining fritters. Serve hot with aïoli (page 108), or with greens like creamed leek tops (page 120).

Kimchi

Fried Rice

This is not your average thrown-together fried rice, but rather a decadent example of the heights of deliciousness this leftover-liberating base can achieve. Jose Mendin combines leftover rice (from yesterday's takeout or Sunday's meal prep) with confit pork belly, caramelized pineapple, kimchi, and vegetables, and—just in case that's not enough to tempt your palate—slides a poached egg on top. Spicy, sweet, and savory, this dish might take a little more time to prepare, but the results are worth every minute.

YIELD: 4 SERVINGS

CONFIT PORK BELLY:
3½ ounces pork belly
2 cups duck fat
2 cups vegetable oil

CARAMELIZED PINEAPPLE:
¼ cleaned pineapple, cut into 1-inch thick steaks

FRIED RICE:
2 tablespoons vegetable oil
1 clove garlic, sliced
2 ounces confited pork belly leftovers, sliced into strips
2 tablespoons kimchi
¼ cup green peas
¼ cup snow peas
2 cups leftover cooked white rice
3 teaspoons kimchi pickling liquid
2 teaspoons soy sauce
4 eggs
4 teaspoons sliced scallions
4 teaspoons white sesame seeds

Make the confit pork belly: heat your oven to 220°F. In a casserole or oven-safe dish, add the duck fat and vegetable oil. Place the pork belly in the dish and submerge it in the oil and fat. Cook the pork belly for 4 hours until tender. Let cool in the fat.

Make the caramelized pineapple: heat a plancha or well-greased cast-iron skillet over medium-high heat. Sear the pineapple steaks in the pan until caramelized, about 2 minutes. Flip and sear on the other side until caramelized, about 2 minutes more. Remove to a cutting board to cool. Once the pineapple is cool enough to handle, cut the steaks into 1-inch cubes. Set aside.

Make the fried rice: in a wok set over medium-high heat, add the vegetable oil. Add the garlic and cook until toasted, about 1 minute. Add the confit pork belly and cook for 2 minutes until it's brown on all sides, stirring occasionally. Add the kimchi, green peas, and snow peas and stir together. Add the rice and let it toast on one side. Slowly add the kimchi pickling liquid and soy sauce and stir well to combine. Add the caramelized pineapple.

Bring a large pot of water to a boil. Add a tablespoon of vinegar. Working one at a time, crack the egg into a small bowl. Drop the egg into the simmering water and poach until the white is cooked through, about 2 to 3 minutes.

Top the rice with the poached eggs, scallions, and white sesame seeds and serve.

Leftover
Doughnut Crème Brûlée

It's hard for us to imagine a scenario where "leftover doughnuts" is a problem, but Lisa Carlson and Carrie Summer faced this conundrum daily after making batches of their signature Indian-spiced miniature doughnuts. Fortunately, their solution is a creamy, luscious dessert that works with any bit of stale bread or leftover pastries, like challah, brioche, croissants, or Danish. The love child of a crème brûlée and bread pudding, this recipe folds the doughnuts in a spiced and sweetened custard, then bakes the whole mixture off until it's just set. Carlson and Summer recommend serving it warm with ice cream, or by the spoonful straight from the refrigerator.

YIELD: 6 TO 8 SERVINGS

4 cups whole milk
4 eggs
½ cup honey or maple syrup
½ teaspoon cinnamon
½ teaspoon vanilla extract
½ teaspoon rose water extract, optional
¼ teaspoon ground nutmeg
¼ teaspoon ground coriander
Pinch sea salt
20 small day-old doughnuts
    or 6 large doughnuts
    (about 6 cups doughnut chunks)
Soft-whipped cream or ice cream
    for serving

Preheat the oven to 350°F.
    Combine half of the milk with the eggs, honey or syrup, cinnamon, vanilla, rose water (if using), nutmeg, coriander, and sea salt in a blender and process until combined. Transfer to a large bowl and add the remaining milk. Stir to combine.
    Fill a shallow 9×12-inch baking pan with the doughnuts. Pour the custard over the doughnuts and let sit for 10 minutes so the doughnuts soak up the liquid. Transfer the pan to the oven and bake for 35 to 40 minutes, or until the sides are firm but the middle is jiggly. Let the pan rest on the counter for 10 minutes. Serve either warm with a dollop of soft-whipped cream or ice cream, or refrigerate for at least 60 minutes and serve cold.

Bubble and Squeak

Nick Leahy adored this British standby as a child, and the dish has since become a beloved staff meal at his restaurant. Leahy also considers it the ultimate leftover utilizer: day-old mashed potatoes are mixed with vegetables, fried in butter, and served with a fried egg on top. It's traditionally made with cabbage (which "bubbles" and "squeaks" as it fries, hence the name), but Leahy assures that it can be a vessel for whatever veg is taking up space in your fridge.

YIELD: 6 SERVINGS

6 tablespoons butter
½ medium onion, diced
1 cup leftover mashed potatoes
½ cup leftover vegetables (such as cabbage, broccoli, Brussels sprouts, carrots, turnips, rutabaga, etc.), chopped
1 egg, plus 6 more eggs for serving
Salt and pepper to taste

In a sauté pan set over medium heat, melt the butter. Add the onions and cook them slowly until they are caramelized, about 10 minutes. Transfer the caramelized onions to a large bowl and add the mashed potatoes, leftover chopped vegetables, and 1 egg. Season to taste with salt and pepper. Be sure to keep any melted butter in the sauté pan.

Form the mixture into small patties about ½-inch-thick. Return the pan to medium heat and fry patties until golden brown and crispy on both sides, about 2 minutes.

Heat a large nonstick pan over medium heat. Working in batches if needed, crack the remaining eggs over the pan and reduce the heat to low. Cover with a lid and let cook for 2 minutes. Top each fried patty with a sunny-side up egg and serve.

VARIATIONS:
— Bread the vegetables in panko crumbs for a crunchier texture.
— Dip the patties in a little grated Parmesan for a cheese crust.
— Add a little chopped, crispy bacon to the bubbles mixture.
— Add fresh jalapeños, chile flakes, curry powder, or fresh herbs.

5.

Prolonged
&
Preserved

Kombucha

At Kaimuki Superette, Ed Kenney pulls in locals for his irresistible "sandwiches and sundries," but true devotées return for the ever-changing kombucha offerings. Fortunately, this fermented tea–based drink is both good for the gut, and good for the shop's bottom line, since it works as an easy outlet for fruit and vegetable peels and scraps, reducing waste and overhead.

Note: to make the kombucha, you'll have to purchase a scoby (symbiotic culture of bacteria and yeast), or acquire one from a fellow homemade kombucha enthusiast. This is a one time purchase from your natural foods store. It's rolled over from each batch of kombucha to the next. As it grows, it can be split to make larger batches or shared with friends who want to make kombucha at home.

YIELD: 2 GALLONS

2 gallons water
2 cups raw sugar
3 tablespoons organic black tea leaves
    (wrapped in cheesecloth)
    or 4 store-bought tea bags
1 scoby
2 feet cheesecloth
1 cup fruit or vegetable trimmings*

First ferment: in a large pot, bring water to boil and add sugar. Allow to cool to 180°F. Add tea satchel (or tea bags) and steep for 10 minutes. Remove the satchel or bags and let the tea cool to room temperature.

Place the tea and scoby in a clean glass container and cover with cheesecloth to allow the liquid to degas. Store in a cool, dark place for 2 weeks. (This step develops the beneficial bacteria and tangy acidity.)

Strain out the scoby and 1 cup of kombucha to be used in your next batch of kombucha. If you are not ready to immediately roll into another batch, the scoby will live for 2 months in the refrigerator stored with the cup of kombucha in a sealed container.

Second ferment: split the kombucha into four ½-gallon mason jars. To each jar, add approximately 1 cup of fruit or vegetable scraps, herbs, and/or spices—this is where you can get creative, although some helpful suggestions are listed below. Cover jars tightly with lids. Leave jars out in a cool, dark place for 2 to 3 days, making sure to burp each jar every day (i.e., loosen the lid briefly) to release gas. (This step infuses flavor into the beverage and forms the effervescence.)

Strain the kombucha and enjoy over ice or in your favorite cocktail. Keep refrigerated for up to 14 days.

*FRUIT AND VEGETABLE TRIMMINGS THAT WORK WELL:
Pineapple cores
Mango pits
Guava skins
Citrus pulp and rinds
Overripe berries
Wilting herbs
Herb stems
Apple or pear cores
Scraped vanilla pods
Coffee beans
Ginger or turmeric trimmings
Melon rinds
Spices
Celery trimmings
Carrot peels
Cucumber seeds
Corncobs
Fennel fronds

Kitchen Scrap Kimchi

According to chef Jason Weiner, stems, cores, and leaves that remain after making kale salad or stuffed cabbage are a veritable treasure trove of flavor. Weiner takes the scraps and transforms them into the base of spicy, good-for-your-gut kimchi— a flavor-packed condiment that you might just want to throw into your next salad bowl for an unexpected Korean kick.

YIELD: 3 CUPS

4 cups cores, stems, and outer leaves of cabbage, kale, chard, beet, or any other greens you have on hand, roughly chopped
1 cup kosher salt
10 to 15 garlic cloves
1 bunch scallions, chopped
1 cup gochugaru (Korean chile powder)
1 cup thinly sliced onion
½ cup sliced Asian pear
½ cup daikon radish, peeled and roughly grated
¼ cup ginger, peeled and chopped
¼ cup fish sauce
2 tablespoons sugar

Toss the greens' cores, stems, and leaves in a large bowl with the salt. Transfer the mixture to a large colander and place the bowl underneath. Let sit overnight on the counter.

The next day, rinse the greens under cold water and pat dry. Transfer to a large bowl and add the remaining ingredients. Mix to combine. Pack the kimchi in clean jars or ziplock bags at room temperature for 2 to 3 days, then refrigerate. The kimchi will keep for 10 to 12 days in the refrigerator.

Savory Granola

Chef Marco Canora's salty, spicy version of this sweet breakfast staple can be used in the same way you would sweeter granolas—as a topping for yogurt or straight from the container as a snack. It's the perfect vehicle for grape tomatoes or sungold tomatoes you want to preserve a little longer. The recipe works best with small tomatoes so that they become raisinlike, but if you have larger tomatoes, cut them up into 1-inch pieces before drying them out. The granola will last about 2 weeks stored in a sealed container.

YIELD: 2 QUARTS

1 or 2 pints of small heirloom tomatoes
3 cups old-fashioned oats
½ cup plus 2 tablespoons almond flour
1 cup Marcona almonds, roughly
     chopped
½ cup extra-virgin olive oil
2 cloves garlic, peeled and crushed

½ teaspoon red pepper flakes
½ cup packed fresh basil leaves
½ cup barley malt syrup
¼ cup dark brown sugar
Zest of 1 lemon, finely grated
1 teaspoon freshly ground black pepper
1 teaspoon sea salt

Prepare the tomatoes: preheat oven to 200°F. Spread the tomatoes in a single layer on a parchment-lined baking sheet. Bake for 8 to 10 hours until most of the moisture is removed and they appear similar to raisins.

Make the granola: preheat the oven to 350°F. Stir oats and almond flour together. Spread on a baking sheet and toast for 15 minutes, until the oats become fragrant. Turn the oven down to 275°F.

While the oats are toasting, bring the olive oil, garlic, and red pepper flakes to a boil. Turn off the heat and stir in the basil leaves. Cover, and let steep for 30 minutes.

In a large mixing bowl, combine barley malt syrup, brown sugar, lemon zest, pepper, and sea salt. When the oil is done steeping, strain it through a fine mesh sieve into the barley syrup mixture, and stir together well.

Pour toasted oat mix and chopped almonds into the same bowl and stir them together until the oats and nuts are coated. Spread the granola onto a baking sheet and return it to the oven for 20 minutes, stirring the granola and turning the pan 180 degrees halfway through. The granola should look dark brown and smell fragrant and toasty. Once it is cool, it should no longer be sticky. If it is, lower the temperature of the oven a bit, and return the sheet for about 10 more minutes. When the granola is cool, break it up into smaller clusters. Mix in the tomato raisins. Store the granola in airtight containers at room temperature.

Pineapple Soda

Don't judge a book by its cover—or a pineapple by its prickly skin. Chef Jamie Simpson creates a pineapple soda based on a recipe from one of his cooks, whose Puerto Rican grandmother used to make the drink on her back porch. Fortunately, this recipe is home kitchen–friendly, no tropical island required. The bubbles arise when the yeast of the peels and leaves consumes the sugars in the water, creating a natural, irresistible carbonated beverage.

YIELD: 1 GALLON SODA

1 gallon distilled water
1 cup organic cane sugar
Peel of 1 whole pineapple
2 pineapple leaves

In a 6-quart pot, bring the water and sugar to a boil. Allow the water to cool somewhat, until it has gone down to around 95°F. Pour the water into a sterile jar or glass container and gently place the raw pineapple peels and leaves into the container. Cover with coffee filters and secure with a rubber band but do not seal the container. (The yeast from the leaves and skin will consume the sugars in the water and ferment, producing carbon dioxide.)

Allow the tea to ferment for about 1 week until you see very little activity in the water in terms of gas production. Strain and transfer to a sealed container like a swing-top bottle or mason jar with new lids. Store for 1 day at room temperature and then transfer to a refrigerator for up to 2 weeks. Degas the jars weekly to release excess gas buildup. Be careful when handling—always open over a sink!

Jamaican Pickled Onions

When it comes to pantry staples, pickling liquid may not be on your list, but Kwame Williams thinks it's a worthy addition. He keeps it on hand to rescue any overripe veggies languishing in the bottom of the crisper. Take this recipe, which transforms any orphaned alliums into a Jamaican-style condiment packed with allspice and peppery heat, and destined for sandwiches, salads, seafood, and more. So next time you encounter past-its-prime produce— start pickling!

YIELD: 2 CUPS

3 cups water
1½ cups apple cider vinegar
¾ cup sugar
¾ teaspoon whole allspice
¾ teaspoon whole black peppercorns
½ Scotch bonnet pepper (optional)
1 large red onion (or other onion you have on hand), thinly sliced into half-moons

Combine all ingredients except the onion in a stainless steel saucepan. Bring mixture to a boil and remove from heat. Let sit for 10 minutes.

Place the onions in an airtight container or jar. Pour 2 cups warm pickling liquid over the onions until they're completely covered. Let the onions steep for 20 minutes, or until the liquid is cool. Use the pickled onions on a sandwich, on top of a salad, or with seafood or steak.

Note: the same pickling liquid and technique can be used whenever you have an excess of produce from the market or your own garden. Just allow a half hour to an hour of steeping time when it comes to hardy vegetables like carrots or cauliflower.

Quick Pickles

Transform trimmings to pickles in a pinch with this recipe from Jennifer Hill Booker, which uses a simple, spice-filled brine to turn extra veggies into a delicious condiment that's good to go as soon as the pickles have cooled. Dig in immediately, or enjoy a nibble or two at a time—these sweet-and-sour savories are good for up to a year in the fridge.

YIELD: 2 QUARTS

4 cups assorted vegetables (like carrots, bell pepper, onion, cucumber, and cauliflower) cut into 2- to 3-inch pieces

2 cups apple cider vinegar
1 cup white wine vinegar
1 cup water
½ cup dark brown sugar
½ cup sugar
2 tablespoons pickling spice
2 tablespoons kosher or sea salt
1 teaspoon black peppercorns
¼ teaspoon red pepper flakes
5–6 sprigs fresh thyme

Place the vegetables in a large nonreactive bowl. Set aside.

Combine the apple cider vinegar, white wine vinegar, water, brown sugar, sugar, pickling spice, salt, black pepper, red pepper, and thyme in a large stainless steel saucepan over medium heat. Heat until the sugar dissolves and the mixture comes to a boil, about 20 minutes. Taste and adjust sugar or salt, if necessary.

Pour the hot pickling brine over the vegetables. Cover loosely with a kitchen towel or plastic wrap, and allow to cool for about 1 hour.

Transfer the pickled vegetables and brine to a large jar or container and cover with a tight-fitting lid. Store pickles in the refrigerator for up to a year, but they are ready to eat as soon as they cool off.

Peach Pit Vodka

Life's a peach when you've got this recipe in your cocktail collection! Jamie Simpson takes the oft-discarded skins and pits of Georgia's favorite fruit and makes them the base of an infused vodka. Take it as the perfect excuse to mix up a few tipples and get fuzzy.

YIELD: 1 CUP PEACH VODKA

6 peach pits
Skins from 6 peaches
1 cup vodka

Wrap your peach pits in a towel. With a large mallet, crack the pits open over stone or another hard surface.

Transfer the cracked pits and peach skins to a jar and submerge in vodka (or the spirit of your choice).

Allow the vodka to sit out for 1 week. Strain through a coffee filter and use in the cocktail of your choice or simply served chilled on the rocks.

Seasonal Fruit Jams

Chef Emily Luchetti is known for the delicious jams she makes all year and gives as gifts wherever she goes. Her method is tried and true, and incredibly simple. Whether you have an abundance of fresh fruit that you want to preserve, or if it's squished, bruised, and just past its prime, you can turn it into jam. Luchetti's formula is using half the amount of sugar to fruit, plus a squeeze of fresh lemon. Her secret to the freshest tasting jam is to make it in small batches so it cooks quickly, which helps preserve the bright flavor of the fruit.

YIELD: 1½ CUPS

1½ pounds peeled and diced peaches
    (about 5 medium peaches)
1½ cups sugar (12 ounces)
2 tablespoons lemon juice

SPECIAL EQUIPMENT:
Glass jars with metal lids for canning

Place 4 or 5 spoons in the freezer. In a wide pot, combine the peaches, sugar, and lemon juice. Cook over medium heat, stirring often, until the fruit starts to give off its juices and the sugar is dissolved, about 3 minutes. Increase the heat to high and cook for about 15 to 20 minutes, stirring frequently until jam thickens. The timing will depend on the pot, stove, and type of fruit. To test readiness, remove one of the frozen spoons from the freezer and spoon a little jam onto one of them and return to the freezer. Let sit a couple of minutes and then tilt the spoon. If it is runny, then cook the jam another couple of minutes. You want it to be thick, but not too stiff.

When the jam is done, put in containers and store in the refrigerator. To preserve for longer, can jam in sterilized jars.

To sterilize jars, bring a large pot of water to a boil. Lower heat to a simmer and submerge each jar (one at a time) in the simmering water for 5 minutes. Carefully pull out with tongs and set on a clean work space.

Scoop the jam into the sterilized jars, leaving a half-inch of space at the top. Seal with lids and return each jar to the water bath. Simmer for another 10 minutes, then remove.

Place the jars upside down on a dishtowel or counter and allow to cool for several hours and up to overnight. If any lids don't "pop" and seal, place those jars in the refrigerator. The others can be stored at room temperature for up to six months.

Tip: instead of peaches, use sliced, unpeeled nectarines or plums; whole raspberries, blackberries, or blueberries; or chopped strawberries.

Citrus Vinegars

After zesting and juicing citrus, the white domes you're left with don't seem very useful. But those pithy domes still have more flavor to give! At Nick's on Broadway, chef Derek Wagner calls these the "hearts" of the fruit, and uses them to make batches of citrus-infused vinegars that are used in everything from the bar to savory dishes to the pastry kitchen. You will need just enough vinegar to cover the spent citrus, so how much vinegar you make will depend on how much fruit you're using.

YIELD: 1 QUART VINEGAR

4 to 8 lemon hearts (white part that's
    left after the fruit has been zested
    and juiced for other purposes)*
Distilled white vinegar (enough to cover)
Sugar (¾ cup per quart of vinegar)
Kosher salt, to taste

MATERIALS:
Sealable glass jars

Submerge the citrus hearts in plain white vinegar and store them in the refrigerator for at least two weeks (they can soak for longer, but need a minimum of 2 weeks to extract enough flavor).

After two weeks, strain the vinegar into a pot. Add sugar and slowly bring it to a very gentle simmer for three minutes. Taste the vinegar and add salt for seasoning if needed. Allow to cool and pour into jars and refrigerate.

*You can also use lime, orange, tangerine, grapefruit, or other citrus fruits for this recipe.

HOW TO USE YOUR CITRUS VINEGARS:
— In dressings and marinades, like a lemon-rosemary vinaigrette or a tangerine-thyme-honey vinaigrette. Finish dishes like roasted fish or chicken, or simple broccoli or asparagus.
— Add a touch of vinegar to simple syrup, toss with sliced fruit, and serve as dessert.
— Use as you would shrubs to add brightness and acidity to mixed drinks. (You can add a touch more sugar or infuse the vinegar with herbs, if desired).

Preserved Lemons

Make these preserved lemons ahead and save for use in recipes like chef Lahlou's asparagus panna cotta (page 40), then toss the pungent, flavorful citrus into salad dressings, soups, or fish and chicken dishes. While they take a month to make, they will last a year or more in the refrigerator.

¾ cup coarse salt
6 whole lemons, scrubbed thoroughly
½ to 1 cup freshly squeezed lemon juice
     (from about 6 lemons)

Place the salt in a large bowl and set aside. Working one at a time, stand the lemon on its stem end on a cutting board; cut down the center as though you were going to cut it in half, but stop about ½ inch above the stem. Make a perpendicular cut, stopping about ½ inch above the stem, so the lemon is quartered but still intact.

Holding the lemon over the bowl of salt, spread the four quarters open and pack as much salt as you can into the lemon, allowing excess salt to fall back into bowl. You should be able to pack about 2 tablespoons into each lemon. Place lemon, cut-side-up, in a 1-quart sterile, dry glass jar, preferably with a neck that is narrower than the jar, with a lid or a clamp closure. Repeat the process with as many lemons as the jar will hold (you may have to add additional lemons the next day when the lemons are softer). Cover and let stand at room temperature overnight.

The next day, push the lemons down with a clean spoon. Add any remaining lemons, if necessary, keeping in mind you may only be able to add another half or quarter. Add enough lemon juice to the jar to completely submerge the lemons. Cover with the lid until just finger-tight or clamp closed. Place the jar in a dark spot in your home, not in the refrigerator.

Every day, for the next week, turn and shake the jar once a day to redistribute the salt. Add more lemon juice if the lemons are no longer submerged. Let the lemons cure for at least four weeks before using.

Peeling Compotable

You may think banana peels are just for pratfalls, but not only are these cartoon clichés edible, they're pretty irresistible when revamped by Hari Pulapaka. To make this waste-free take on a compote, Pulapaka cooks down the banana skins with citrus rinds, pulp, and juices, warming spices, and a little heat from a habanero. The result is the perfect topper for dinner (think roasted pork) or breakfast (on French toast, pancakes, or mixed into yogurt).

YIELD: APPROXIMATELY 3 CUPS

Skins of 6 bananas, with ends trimmed, roughly chopped
Peel, pulp, and juice of 4 lemons, seeds removed and roughly chopped
Peel, pulp, and juice of 2 oranges, seeds removed and roughly chopped
1 cup apple cider vinegar
1 cup granulated sugar
1 cup water
1 cinnamon stick
1 hot pepper of your choice, such as habanero
1 star anise
Kosher salt to taste
fresh herbs like tarragon, mint, or basil, chopped (optional)

In a heavy-bottomed saucepan, simmer all of the ingredients over low heat for about 1 hour. Remove the hot pepper, cinnamon stick, and star anise. Adjust the level of sugar, acid, and salt. Allow to cool.

Drain the mixture, reserving the liquid. With a hand blender or in a food processor, coarsely blend the mixture by adding as much reserved liquid as required. Do not puree the mixture; you want some texture. Return to low heat until warmed through.

Roasted Vegetable Spread

When it comes to non-fruit preserves, herbs and alliums spring to mind. As Jennifer Hill Booker shows, though, plenty of vegetables shine when turned spreadable. This condiment is a catch-all for less-than-pristine produce, as any visible blemishes disappear when the vegetables are roasted to coax out maximum flavor. Booker pairs naturally sweeter vegetables like squash and zucchini with jalapeños, bell peppers, and herbs for a balanced spread that works well on sandwiches, as a gazpacho garnish, or on its own as a vegetable dip.

YIELD: 4 CUPS

1 medium eggplant, peeled
2 small crook-necked yellow squash
2 small zucchini
1 red bell pepper, seeded
1 red onion, peeled
4 large garlic cloves
1 large jalapeño, halved and seeded
3 tablespoons olive oil
3 teaspoons sea salt
½ teaspoon freshly cracked black pepper
2 tablespoons freshly squeezed lemon juice
2 tablespoons Italian parsley, chopped
1 tablespoon tarragon, chopped

Preheat the oven to 400°F.

Cut the eggplant, squash, zucchini, bell pepper, and onion into 1-inch pieces. Toss in a large bowl with the garlic, jalapeño, olive oil, salt, and pepper.

Spread the vegetables out on 2 baking sheets and place in the oven. Roast until the vegetables are lightly browned and soft; stirring once or twice during cooking, 30 to 45 minutes.

Remove from the oven and cool slightly. Squeeze the lemon juice on top of the baking sheets and place the vegetables in a food mill or food processor and process until vegetables are spreadable, about 1 minute, working in batches if needed. Taste and add more salt and pepper if needed.

Transfer to a bowl and top with the parsley and tarragon. Serve chilled as a sandwich spread, garnish for gazpacho, or vegetable dip.

Victor Albisu

Del Campo, Washington, D.C.; and Taco Bamba, Falls Church, VA
Victor Albisu has more than a decade of experience in fine dining and upscale French, American, and Latin American restaurants. He combines his culinary education with his Latin American heritage to bring a unique style of cuisine to his restaurants Del Campo and Taco Bamba. Victor is a frontline chef for World Central Kitchen, José Andrés's nonprofit that feeds survivors of natural disasters.

Cathal Armstrong

Restaurant Eve, Alexandria, VA
Irish chef Cathal Armstrong's cuisine and philosophy reflect ideas planted in the atypical Dublin household of his childhood, where garlic was used fearlessly and fruits and vegetables were grown in the garden. Opened in 2004, Restaurant Eve is a modern American restaurant that showcases Cathal's playful personal style and deep-rooted commitment to purveyors.

Charleen Badman

FnB, Scottsdale, AZ
As chef and co-owner of the award-winning FnB restaurant in Scottsdale, Charleen Badman is one of Arizona's most celebrated chefs. A four-time James Beard Award nominee for Best Chef: Southwest, Charleen is a master gardener and works with Chef in the Garden, where she is a mentor to young people.

Greg Baker

The Refinery, Tampa, FL
Greg Baker opened the Refinery in 2010 in Tampa, Florida. His menus incorporate the flavors of countrysides across the globe, mixed with classical French technique and the influences of Florida's rich cultural history. Greg is a vocal proponent of sustainable agriculture and fisheries, both in raising public awareness and advocating smart policy on the state and federal levels.

Rick Bayless

Frontera Restaurants, Chicago, IL
Rick Bayless is a multiple James Beard Award–winning, Daytime Emmy-nominated chef, restaurateur, and author of nine celebrated cookbooks on authentic Mexican cuisine. The government of Mexico has bestowed on Rick the Order of the Aztec Eagle—the highest decoration bestowed on foreigners whose work has benefited Mexico and its people.

Abra Berens

Chicago, IL
Abra Berens is the chef at Granor Farm in Three Oaks, Michigan, and author of *Ruffage: A Practical Guide to Vegetable Variations*. She strives to make simple, delicious food that celebrates the Midwest, and believes that the meals we eat should change with the seasons and that the ingredients should come from nearby.

Jennifer Hill Booker

Your Resident Gourmet, Atlanta, GA
Jennifer Hill Booker is a chef, cookbook author of *Field Peas to Foie Gras* and *Dinner Deja Vu*, reality TV personality, culinary educator, and business owner. She is a Georgia Grown Executive Chef for the Georgia Department of Agriculture, the Culinary Explorer for the Georgia Department of Tourism and Travel, and currently sits on the James Beard Foundation Food Waste Advisory Council.

Jamilka Borges

Pittsburgh, PA
After growing up in Puerto Rico, Jamilka Borges made her way to the United States at age twenty, enrolling in the culinary program at the Art Institute of Pittsburgh and establishing herself in the city's fledgling restaurant scene. It was at Bar Marco that Jamilka made

a name for herself, both in Pittsburgh and nationally, earning a 2015 James Beard Award semifinalist nod for Rising Star Chef. She is on the advisory board of 412 Food Rescue.

Amy Brandwein

Centrolina, Washington, D.C.
Amy Brandwein is the chef and owner of Centrolina, a combined seasonal Italian restaurant and market that opened in Washington, D.C., in spring 2015. Amy was a 2017 James Beard Award finalist for Best Chef: Mid-Atlantic and is a 2018 James Beard Award semifinalist for Best Chef: Mid-Atlantic. She has a partnership with DC UrbanGreens.

Katie Button

Cúrate Tapas Bar and Nightbell, Asheville, NC
Katie Button is the James Beard Award–nominated chef and owner of Cúrate Tapas Bar and Nightbell in Asheville, North Carolina, and the author of *Cúrate: Authentic Spanish Food from an American Kitchen.* A passionate proponent in the fight against food waste and hunger, Katie has starred on the Asheville episode of the food waste culinary series *Scraps,* and has joined Food Policy Action in Washington, D.C., to support the Supplemental Nutrition Assistance Program (SNAP). She has worked tirelessly to support Asheville's own MANNA FoodBank and the Haywood Street Congregation Downtown Welcome Table.

Marco Canora

Brodo, Hearth, and Zadie's Oyster Room, New York, NY
Chef, restaurateur, and cookbook author Marco Canora has been doing his part to promote delicious, simple, and healthful food that he believes is everyone's birthright. Since 1996, his cuisine has earned critical acclaim, including the 2017 James Beard Award for Best Chef: New York City, and his Italian-inflected cooking has been hailed as some of the finest this side of the Atlantic.

Lisa Carlson

Chef Shack, Minneapolis, MN
Lisa Carlson is chef and co-owner of Chef Shack, a mobile kitchen serving up some of the tastiest street food in Minneapolis. Lisa's career spans many cities collaborating with some of the world's top chefs, including Daniel Humm, Gray Kunz, and Christian Delouvrier.

Ashley Christensen

Ashley Christensen Restaurants, Raleigh, NC
Ashley Christensen is the chef and owner of seven restaurants in downtown Raleigh, North Carolina. Ashley's cooking and her philosophy of bright, fresh flavors and locally grown, seasonal ingredients have garnered local and national acclaim, and in 2014, Ashley won the James Beard Award for Best Chef: Southeast. In 2017, she and chef Vivian Howard were named Tar Heels of the Year by the *Raleigh News & Observer* for their community leadership.

Joy Crump

FOODĒ, Fredericksburg, VA
Joy Crump is chef and co-owner of FOODĒ, a locally focused restaurant with a weekly shifting menu based on the bounty that regional farmers, meat purveyors, and suppliers have to offer.

Tiffany Derry

Tiffany Derry Concepts, Dallas, TX
Tiffany Derry is the owner of Roots Fried Chicken and Tiffany Derry Concepts. She gained international notoriety on the seventh season of Bravo's *Top Chef* and as a finalist on *Top Chef: All-Stars.* Tiffany also sits on the James Beard Foundation's Impact Programs Advisory Committee and gives back to her local community by participating in programs with the Dallas Independent School District and the North Texas Food Bank.

William Dissen

The Market Place Restaurant, Asheville, NC; and Haymaker, Charlotte, NC
William Dissen is the chef and owner of the Market Place Restaurant, located on Asheville's historic Wall Street, and Haymaker Restaurant in Uptown Charlotte. William is a food policy advocate, serving as a board member on the Appalachian Sustainable Agriculture Project, a culinary diplomat in the American Chef Corps, and as a member of the Monterey Bay Aquarium Blue Ribbon Task Force.

Kirsten Dixon

Winterlake Lodge, Skwentna, AK; and Tutka Bay Lodge, Homer, AK
Kirsten Dixon has been cooking in the backcountry of Alaska for more than twenty years, and has published several cookbooks, including *The Winterlake Lodge Cookbook*. She spends most of her time at Winterlake Lodge, where she frequently teaches cooking classes in the kitchen or gives tours of the herb garden.

Duskie Estes

Zazu Kitchen + Farm and Black Pig Meat Co., Sebastopol, CA
Duskie Estes is an avid farmer and rancher, growing all the ingredients that go into her ribollita, and raising Mangalitsa pigs, babydoll sheep, goats, chickens, heritage turkeys, and rabbits on her farm. In 2001, Duskie and her husband, chef John Stewart, opened Zazu Kitchen + Farm, where she practices "snout-to-tail" cooking.

Elizabeth Falkner

New York, NY
Elizabeth Falkner has worked in and owned restaurants in San Francisco and New York for more than two decades. A 2005 James Beard Award nominee, Elizabeth has appeared on a number of television shows and is the author of two cookbooks, *Demolition Desserts* (2007) and *Cooking Off the Clock* (2012). She is an advocate of mindful cooking and speaks to groups about getting everyone to exercise and to "stay fit to cook."

Paul Fehribach

Big Jones, Chicago, IL
At Big Jones, chef/owner Paul Fehribach's vision is grounded deeply in the rich and diverse heritage that is the Southern kitchen, using the arc of history to bring you food that is as refined as it is down-home satisfying. Paul published *The Big Jones Cookbook* with University of Chicago Press in May 2015.

Kenny Gilbert

Gilbert's Underground Kitchen and Gilbert's Social, Jacksonville, FL
Kenny Gilbert is the chef/owner of Gilbert's Underground Kitchen, Gilbert's Social, Gilbert's Southern Kitchen & Bar, and Gilbert's Hot Chicken, Fish & Shrimp in Jacksonville Beach, and is known for his appearance on season seven of *Top Chef*, in which he was the fan favorite. Gilbert also has his own line of culinary spice blends.

Debbie Gold

Tied House, Chicago, IL
A James Beard Award winner and four-time nominee, Debbie Gold ran the kitchen at Kansas City's The American, receiving national accolades and recognition. Debbie went on to open her own restaurant, 40 Sardines, which was nominated for the James Beard Award for Best New Restaurant, and is now the chef at Tied House in Chicago.

Sarah Grueneberg

Monteverde Restaurant & Pastificio, Chicago, IL
Sarah Grueneberg is head chef and owner of Monteverde Restaurant & Pastificio, and the winner of the 2017 James Beard Award for Best Chef: Great Lakes. Prior to opening Monteverde, Sarah ran the kitchen at the Michelin-starred Spiaggia, and competed on Bravo's *Top Chef*, finishing as runner-up on the ninth season.

Ben Hall	*Russell Street Deli, Detroit, MI*
	Ben Hall is the chef/co-owner of Russell Street Deli in Detroit, which, in addition to its retail business, provides 5,000 gallons of soup each week to specialty grocery stores, soup kitchens, and Detroit public schools.

Evan Hanczor	*Egg Restaurant, Brooklyn, NY*
	Evan Hanczor is the chef at Egg, a farm-to-table, breakfast-focused restaurant in Brooklyn with an outpost in Tokyo and a farm in the Catskills. He is the coauthor, with Egg founder George Weld, of *Breakfast: Recipes to Wake Up For*, and also the creator and curator of Tables of Contents, an edible reading series hosted monthly at Egg. He works on food policy and advocacy with the Chef Action Network and several food-focused nonprofits on both local and global issues.

Howard Hanna	*The Rieger and Ça Va, Kansas City, MO*
	Howard Hanna is chef and co-owner of lauded restaurant Rieger and award-winning Champagne bar Ça Va in Kansas City, Missouri.

Maria Hines	*Maria Hines Restaurants, Seattle, WA*
	Winner of the 2009 James Beard Award for Best Chef: Northwest, Maria Hines has expanded her restaurant group into award-winning and diverse concepts Tilth and Agrodolce. With her intense, unwavering dedication to local farmers and organic ingredients, Maria has had all her restaurants certified organic by the esteemed Oregon Tilth, and is a founding board member of the James Beard Foundation's Chef Action Network.

Mike Isabella	*Mike Isabella Concepts, Washington, D.C.; Bethesda and College Park, MD; Arlington, Fairfax, Merrifield, and Richmond, VA*
	Mike Isabella is the chef and owner of more than a dozen restaurants in Washington, D.C., Maryland, and Virginia, with additional outposts in Nationals Park and Ronald Reagan National Airport. He appeared on the sixth season of *Top Chef, Top Chef: Duels*, and was a runner-up on *Top Chef: All-Stars*.

Jennifer Jasinski	*Bistro Vendôme, Euclid Hall, Rioja, and Stoic & Genuine, Denver, CO*
	Winner of the 2013 James Beard Award for Best Chef: Southwest, Jennifer Jasinski is the chef/owner of five celebrated restaurants in Denver. Jennifer sits on the James Beard Foundation Impact Programs Advisory Committee and on the Good Food Media Network Culinary Advisory Board.

Sara Jenkins	*Porsena, New York, NY; and Nina June, Rockport, ME*
	Sara Jenkins is the chef/owner of New York City's Porsena, and Nina June, located in the seaside village of Rockport, Maine. She is the author of two cookbooks, *Olives and Oranges: Recipes and Flavor Secrets from Italy, Spain, Cyprus, and Beyond*, and *The Four Seasons of Pasta*. Growing up on a Tuscan farm she learned the importance of frugality and the deep satisfaction one feels from getting the maximum usage out of an ingredient.

Ed Kenney	*Town Hospitality Group, Honolulu, HI*
	Ed Kenney is a successful restaurateur with a strong commitment to telling stories through food. Ed's four restaurants—Town, Kaimuki Superette, Mud Hen Water, and Mahina & Sun's—are lively gathering places guided by the mantra "local first, organic whenever possible, with aloha always."

Josh Kulp

Honey Butter Fried Chicken, Chicago, IL
Josh Kulp is cofounder and co-chef of Chicago's decade-old Sunday Dinner Club, and the fast-casual Honey Butter Fried Chicken. Both businesses emphasize environmental sustainability as well as improving working conditions in restaurants. Josh and his partner Christine Cikowski have served on the Mayor's Task Force for Working Families, and have traveled to Washington, D.C., to lobby congress on labor issues as restaurant owners.

Mourad Lahlou

Mourad, San Francisco, CA
After earning a master's degree in macroeconomics, Morocco native Mourad Lahlou opened his first restaurant, Kasbah, in San Rafael, California. In 2001, Mourad opened Aziza in San Francisco, earning three and a half stars from the *San Francisco Chronicle*. Now at his third restaurant, Mourad, he has garnered praise for his family-style fare, which melds modern techniques with tradition.

Nick Leahy

Saltyard, Atlanta, GA
Nick Leahy is best known for his work at Saltyard, a tapas-style restaurant in Atlanta. While always experimenting with international flavors, Nick is also passionate about using local, organic ingredients whenever possible, and works daily with local farmers to source his menu.

Jay Lippin

Crabtree's Kittle House, Chappaqua, NY
Jay Lippin was first appointed executive chef of Crabtree's Kittle House in 1991. He went on to run kitchens in New York City and Westchester, open his own restaurant, and win an episode of the Food Network's *Chopped* before returning to the Kittle House in 2012 to expand the venerable restaurant's role as farm-to-table pioneer by supporting multiple organizations focused on sustainable, humane food practices.

Jordan Lloyd

Bartlett Pear Inn, Easton, MD
Jordan Lloyd worked under Thomas Keller, Christian Delouvrier, and the late Michel Richard before revamping the Bartlett Pear Inn in his hometown of Easton, MD. In 2016, Jordan and his wife, Alice, closed the restaurant portion of the business to focus on their children and operating their Eastern Shore bed-and-breakfast. While continuing to cook throughout the D.C. area, Jordan supports Chesapeake Harvest, a company guided by farmers, harvesters, and watermen of his community.

Emily Luchetti

Big Night Restaurant Group, San Francisco, CA
Emily Luchetti is a multiple James Beard Award–winning pastry chef and cookbook author who has helped define what great pastry in America means. Emily is the Chief Pastry Officer for the Big Night Restaurant Group in San Francisco. She has served on the James Beard Foundation Board of Trustees for the past ten years.

Matt McClure

The Hive, Bentonville, AR
Since joining the opening team of the Hive at the 21c Museum Hotel in Bentonville in 2012, Matthew McClure has showcased the refined, country cuisine of the high South. Matt's cooking highlights local ingredients and traditions from northwest Arkansas and emphasizes the full utilization of ingredients to maximize flavor and minimize waste. Matt is a multiple James Beard Award semifinalist, an ambassador for No Kid Hungry, an advocate for sustainability, a husband, father, and outdoorsman.

Jose Mendin	*Food Comma Hospitality Group and Pubbelly Boys, Miami, FL* Jose Mendin is the chef/co-owner of Food Comma Hospitality Group, a Miami-based restaurant group. He is a five-time James Beard Award semifinalist for Best Chef: Southeast.
Mary Sue Milliken	*Border Grill, Los Angeles and Las Vegas* Mary Sue Milliken is co-chef/owner of Border Grill with Susan Feniger, serving modern Mexican food in Los Angeles and Santa Monica, California; Las Vegas at Mandalay Bay Resort & Casino; and on the Border Grill Truck. Mary Sue is a preeminent ambassador of authentic Mexican cuisine, setting the standard for gourmet Mexican fare for over two decades and coauthoring five cookbooks. She is on the board of No Kid Hungry.
Seamus Mullen	*El Colmado and Tertulia, New York, NY* Seamus Mullen is a chef, restaurateur, and cookbook author known for his inventive yet approachable Spanish cuisine, and his expertise on health and wellness. Seamus opened his first restaurant, Tertulia, in 2011, which was awarded two stars from the *New York Times* and was a finalist for the James Beard Award for Best New Restaurant. In 2013, he opened El Colmado, a Spanish tapas and wine bar.
Patrick Mulvaney	*Mulvaney's B&L, Sacramento, CA* A leading public policy advocate on the national stage, Patrick Mulvaney is one of the people working to make Sacramento the "farm-to-fork" capital of the country. In addition to his work at Mulvaney's B&L, Patrick is a board member of the Foundation for California Community Colleges; works with the Edible Sac High Program at Sacramento High School; and Plates Cafe, a workforce training program.
Mark Noguchi	*Pili Group, Honolulu, HI* Mark Noguchi's dedication to empowering his community through food and education has made him a leader in Hawaii's sustainable food movement. Mark's Pili Group focuses on the connection between community, education, and food. His greatest accomplishment is being a father to his two daughters and husband to his wife, Amanda.
Mario Pagán	*Mario Pagán Restaurant and Sage Steak Loft, San Juan, Puerto Rico* Mario Pagán is the chef and owner of Mario Pagán Restaurant and Sage Steak Loft in San Juan, Puerto Rico, and executive chef at Dorado Beach Resort & Golf Club in Dorado, Puerto Rico. Mario is also the author of two books, *Cocinas del Mundo CARIBE* and *La Gran Cocina Caribeña y sus 12 Grandes Chefs*.
Hari Pulapaka	*Cress Restaurant, DeLand, FL* Hari Pulapaka, a native of Mumbai, India, teaches mathematics at Stetson University and is also a classically trained chef. When he is not teaching, he is at Cress, a pioneering restaurant in DeLand that he owns and operates with his wife Jenneffer. Beyond the food waste program at Cress, Hari teaches about food waste-related problems and solutions.
Steven Satterfield	*Miller Union, Atlanta, GA* James Beard Award–winning chef Steven Satterfield is executive chef and co-owner of Miller Union, a celebrated, seasonally driven restaurant in Atlanta's Westside neighborhood. In 2015, Steven released his first cookbook, *Root to Leaf*, to critical acclaim.

Jonathon Sawyer	*Team Sawyer Restaurants, Cleveland, OH*
	As a proud Clevelander, James Beard Award–winning chef Jonathon Sawyer has worked tirelessly to help elevate the culinary landscape of his hometown with his distinctive restaurant concepts. Jonathon is a tireless supporter of the green movement, local agriculture, and sustainable businesses both in northeast Ohio and around the country.
Jamie Simpson	*The Culinary Vegetable Institute at the Chef's Garden, Milan, OH*
	Chef Jamie Simpson is the executive chef liaison of the Culinary Vegetable Institute at the Chef's Garden. He has earned a reputation for the application and knowledge of vegetables at every stage of their life. At CVI, he designs dishes around what is available on the farm that day in keeping with his commitment to micro-seasonal cooking.
Ana Sortun	*Oleana, Sarma, and Sofra Bakery and Café, Boston, MA*
	Ana Sortun opened Oleana in Boston in 2001, and was named Best Chef: Northeast by the James Beard Foundation in 2005. She went on to open Sofra Bakery and Café, and co-owns Sarma in Somerville. She is the author of two cookbooks, *Spice: Flavors of the Eastern Mediterranean* and *Soframiz: Vibrant Middle Eastern Recipes from Sofra Bakery and Cafe* with Maura Kilpatrick. Ana is known for bringing Middle Eastern flavors into the mainstream through her passion for Turkish cooking, spices, and her husband Chris Kurth of Siena Farms's organic vegetables.
Carrie Summer	*Chef Shack, Minneapolis, MN*
	Carrie Summer is chef and co-owner of Chef Shack. Carrie and her business partner, chef Lisa Carlson, each have twenty years of experience working in notable fine-dining kitchens in Minneapolis, New York, and San Francisco.
Sam Talbot	New York, NY
	Sam Talbot is a celebrated chef, healthy living expert, and philanthropist. He is the author of the cookbook/memoir *The Sweet Life: Diabetes without Boundaries* and *100% Real*. He cofounded a nonprofit with Nick Jonas called Beyond Type 1 that focuses on type 1 diabetes. He is active on issues surrounding food waste, fighting hunger, and keeping our oceans safe and populated for generations to come.
Bill Telepan	*Oceana, New York, NY*
	Bill Telepan is one of New York's leaders in sourcing quality ingredients from small farms and local purveyors. Prior to becoming executive chef at Oceana, Bill was the chef and owner of the critically acclaimed, Michelin-starred Telepan Restaurant on Manhattan's Upper West Side. He is the director of sustainability at the Institute of Culinary Education and executive chef of Wellness in the Schools.
Bryant Terry	*Museum of the African Diaspora, San Francisco, CA*
	Bryant Terry is a 2015 James Beard Foundation Leadership Award–winning chef, educator, and author renowned for his activism to create a healthy, just, and sustainable food system. He is currently the inaugural chef in residence at the Museum of the African Diaspora (MoAD) in San Francisco.
Derek Wagner	*Nick's on Broadway, Providence, RI*
	Derek Wagner is the chef/owner of Nick's on Broadway, an ever-evolving, seasonally inspired, locally supported restaurant focused on integrity, soulfully driven food, and sincere service. Whatever he cannot produce or grow at Nick's, he tries to source

carefully, thoughtfully, and locally whenever possible. Derek is the co-chair of Chefs Collaborative and a passionate advocate for building community and a healthier, more sustainable food system. He dedicates time and effort to creating awareness and impact on important issues such as reducing food waste, fighting food insecurity, better meat practices, and seafood advocacy.

Levon Wallace	*Gray & Dudley at the 21c Museum Hotel, Nashville, TN*

Gray & Dudley at the 21c Museum Hotel, Nashville, TN
Levon Wallace is executive chef at Gray & Dudley at the 21c Museum Hotel in Nashville. A California native, Levon has become a self-declared "wannabilly," grafting his roots with Tennessee's and making Gray & Dudley one of the most exciting places to eat in Nashville. He is an active member and supporter of No Kid Hungry and Hunters for the Hungry, and has worked on food waste initiatives with other Nashville chefs and the mayor of Nashville.

Nick Wallace

Historic King Edward Hotel, Jackson, MS
Nick Wallace is the executive chef at the Historic King Edward Hotel, and is a leader in redefining the Southern food experience, blending his Mississippi family-farm origins with sophisticated French techniques to create exceptional dining experiences.

Jason Weiner

Almond, Bridgehampton, NY, and New York, NY
Jason Weiner is the executive chef and proprietor of Almond, an American bistro with locations in Manhattan and Bridgehampton, New York. Jason serves hearty, seasonal dishes that reflect farm-to-table roots and highlight local ingredients.

Matthew Weingarten

Dig Inn, New York, NY
Matthew Weingarten is the chief culinary officer for Dig Inn, an NYC-based restaurant group that serves seasonal, vegetable-forward dishes. At Dig Inn, Matthew oversees the group's sourcing practices and menu development, as well as the chefs running their kitchens. He is the former chair of Chefs Collaborative's board of directors, helping to develop programming that inspires and educates food professionals as frontline advocates for a better food system.

Cathy Whims

Nostrana and Oven and Shaker, Portland, OR
Cathy Whims is executive chef and owner of Nostrana, a rustic Italian restaurant specializing in the regional cuisines of Italy and using ingredients provided by many of the best farmers, cheese makers, and meat producers in the Northwest. Cathy and her husband, David West, are also partners at Oven and Shaker, a modern urban saloon specializing in wood-fired pizzas.

Kwame Williams

Vital Restaurant, Montclair, NJ
An alum of Minton's in Harlem, in 2014, Jamaican-American Kwame Williams and his two sisters launched Vital in Montclair, New Jersey, a Jamaican restaurant that boasts healthful, vibrant food. In 2016, Kwame and his sisters opened their second concept, Freetown Café, to nourish the often-overlooked Newark community.

Lee Anne Wong

Koko Head Café, Honolulu, HI
Lee Anne Wong is the chef and owner of Koko Head Cafeě in Honolulu, Hawaii, and Sweetcatch Poke in New York City. After competing on Bravo's *Top Chef*, Lee Anne worked as supervising culinary producer for the show. She also serves as the executive chef for Hawaiian Airlines.

The James Beard Foundation would like to thank the following individuals for their work on this project:

All of the chefs who participate in James Beard Foundation programs—particularly those who've been involved in the JBF Chef's Boot Camp for Policy and Change—for their generosity of spirit, talent, and time; and to the chefs who contributed both their recipes and wisdom to this project.

Our colleagues at the James Beard Foundation, especially Mitchell Davis, Kris Moon, and Katherine Miller, whose work inspired this project and who were instrumental in bringing this idea to fruition. Special thanks to JBF editorial director Alison Tozzi Liu, who oversaw this project and contributed much of the editing, writing, and food styling; and the JBF media team Elena North-Kelly, Maggie Borden, Hilary Deutsch, Eden Kanowitz, and Kate Dobday for your passion, energy, and attention to every detail. And to Susan Ungaro and Clare Reichenbach for your leadership, past and present.

The incredibly talented and creative photography team, Keirnan Monaghan and Theo Vamvounakis, as well as food stylists Michelle Gatton and Maggie Ruggiero.

Our recipe testers, Stephanie Bourgeois, Patty Nusser, Elizabeth Laseter, Jana Harrison, Victoria Jordan Rodriguez, and Izabela Wojcik.

Copy editor Amy Zavatto, and designers Sonya Dyakova and Gabriella Voyias of Atelier Dyakova.

Caitlin Leffel, our editor, for expertly guiding and encouraging us throughout the process of putting this book together, and to Rizzoli publisher Charles Miers for believing in this project.

COLOPHON

Design by Atelier Dyakova

Photographs © Keirnan Monaghan and Theo Vamvounakis

Printed in China

ISBN: 978-0-8478-6278-8

Library of Congress Control Number: 2018942775